KNOWING

GOD THROUGH

FASTING

ELMER TOWNS

Destiny Image® Publishers, Inc.
P.O. Box 310
Shippensburg, PA 17257-0310

"Speaking to the Purposes of God for This Generation
and for the Generations to Come"

ISBN 0-7684-2069-5

For Worldwide Distribution
Printed in the U.S.A.

This book and all other Destiny Image, Revival Press, MercyPlace,
Fresh Bread, Destiny Image Fiction, and Treasure House books are
available at Christian bookstores and distributors worldwide.

For a U.S. bookstore nearest you, call 1-800-722-6774.
For more information on foreign distributors, call 717-532-3040.
Or reach us on the Internet:
www.destinyimage.com

CONTENTS

FOREWORD

One of my most treasured friendships is the one I share with Elmer Towns. Friendships flourish in an environment of shared interests and mutual trust. The thing Dr. Towns and I share is our pursuit of God, that inner drive and desire to know Him and be anointed by Him in the ministry of writing.

One of the highest compliments I've ever been paid came from Dr. Towns when he commented that he felt I had been anointed to write. He said that he wanted an anointing of God to come upon him to write spiritually so that when people read his writing, they feel the presence of God. He asked me to pray for him. Even though this conversation took place via telephone, the prayer was heard in the heavens. I asked God to speak to the heart of every reader—and when I read the manuscript of *Knowing God through Fasting*, I felt His presence in the pages and knew He had answered our prayer.

You now hold in your hand the finished product. Some books will try and tell you how to know God from a theological perspective. Other books will try to explain what knowing God really means and give you practical applications for your life. This book is different. It creates hunger for His presence. And, I join the author, in praying that you, the reader, may know God more intimately than you ever have before.

Knowing God is not difficult. You do not need some ancient or modern mantra. There is no special formula. Elmer Towns has made knowing God as simple as tasting...waiting...coming...drinking...looking...resting. The answer to knowing God is not found in a pilgrimage to some sacred location. You do not come to know Him by the study of deep theological texts. You learn to know God by looking within your heart, and opening its doors to Him. The first chapter simply says to know God is to empty your heart of self, desire and self-pride. When you empty yourself to God, He will fill you.

Tommy Tenney

Author of *The God Chasers*

INTRODUCTION

As I ended a 40-day fast, the publisher asked me, "What is the biggest answer to prayer you got from fasting?" I didn't know how to answer him because I didn't get a spectacular answer to prayer. When I finally admitted I didn't receive an answer, he then asked, "Well, why did you put yourself through this agony for 40 days?"

Again I was perplexed, because it wasn't agony, but a wonderful experience. I answered, "Fasting helped me know God, day by day; I encountered Him like never before."

"Write that in a book," he quickly responded. I did. It was a book entitled *God Encounters*, relating stories of how people in the Bible encountered God and how contemporary people can encounter God. It's a good book, but it didn't do what I intended. I wanted you, the reader, to personally meet God as you read its pages. But that didn't happen. The book merely described beneficial examples of *others* who experienced God.

This book, *Knowing God Through Fasting*, is written so *you* will experience God as you read its pages. That's my prayer.

As I wrote this book, I talked to God. Now I want you to talk to Him as you read. Sometimes I talked out loud, sometimes it was internal—subvocal talking—more active than thinking. I talked to God in my mind. Will you talk to God as you read?

In addition, I touched God as I wrote this book. No, not with a hand or finger. But it was still like touching someone physically; I knew inwardly what I experienced. That's the sensation I felt as I wrote this book. I touched God. Will you also try to touch Him as you read?

Also, I heard God talking to me as I wrote this book. No, not with an audible voice. When someone talks to me, I inwardly know what he or she says because I hear him or her with my ears. Instead, as I wrote this book, I inwardly knew what God was saying to me because I experienced *spirit-hearing*. God was talking to me. Will you also try to touch Him as you read?

But more importantly than my touching God, He touched me. The God of the universe came into my room. I could feel His presence, but not see Him with my eyes. I knew He was there, just as surely as I know my wife sits across from me when we eat a meal. God touched me.

Before you begin reading this book, will you pray, "Touch me, O God, as I read this book"?

This book doesn't explain a lot about the methods of fasting. If you need instructions, read *Fasting For Spiritual Breakthrough*, by Elmer Towns, Regal Books, 1996. It will teach you the nine biblical fasts and the various ways to fast for different problems that you face. If you need instruction in how to pray, consult the book, *Prayer Partners*, by Elmer Towns, Regal Books, 2002.

This book that you hold in your hands attempts to tell you how to know God intimately. It's written to create a yearning in your spirit to know God and to satisfy that desire as you read. When you fast, you should get hungry and thirsty. My prayer is that this book will make you hunger and thirst after righteousness. If it succeeds, then I point you to Jesus Christ who alone can satisfy your desires.

To the glory of God.

Elmer Towns

Chapter 1

EMPTYING

Pour out your heart before Him: God is a refuge for us
(Psalm 62:8b).
...I will pour out My Spirit upon all flesh (Joel
2:28a).
Be filled with the Spirit (Ephesians 5:18b).
...they were all filled with the Holy Spirit (Acts 4:31a
NIV).

A s Elijah the prophet entered the town of Zarephath,
he searched for a certain person. God had told him
to go there to live with a widow. "Why a widow?" the gruff
old prophet might have asked. For widows didn't usually
have much food, especially in those days; as a famine
consumed that region, people were starving. Even the
king had dispatched exploratory teams to find food and
green pastureland for his cattle. When Elijah first met the

widow gathering sticks at the gate of the city he commanded her, "Make me first some bread."

But the widow protested, "I have only enough oil and meal for my son and me. Then we will die."

Elijah persisted, "Make me first, then you will eat" (see 1 Kings 17:1-16).

In this powerful Scripture principle, God says you must give away to receive. When your supply becomes empty, trust God because then He can fill you. In other words, if you want to be filled with God, you must first empty yourself.

As a testimony to the vibrancy of her faith, the widow obeyed. She fed Elijah first, then discovered there was enough left over for her and her son...but not for just one meal; there was a reoccurring daily replenishing of the oil and grain. She lived because she gave all to God. The Lord continually fills those who are empty. *Lord, I empty myself again; fill me.*

Empty pots. After old Elijah was gone, a younger prophet named Elisha had a similar experience (see 2 Kings 4:1-7). A widow came to him who was being threatened with bankruptcy because she couldn't pay her bills. The creditors had threatened to throw her two sons into servitude to satisfy the widow's debt. She appealed to the prophet Elisha for help and informed him that she had only one little pot of oil left. The prophet told her to borrow as many empty pots as she could find. She was not told to borrow pots full of oil, nor was she told to borrow just oil. She was to collect empty pots, "*not a few*" (see

2 Kings 4:3). That phrase meant she was to get as many as possible.

When the empty pots, pans, jugs, and vessels were scattered out on the floors of her house, everything was ready. Why did the prophet say, *"empty pots"*? She would use the one pot of oil to fill the empty ones. She then sold the oil to pay her debt. In application, you must bring an empty life to Jesus Christ for Him to fill. *Lord, I bring as many "empty pots" as I can find.*

Empty yourself to be filled with God. Paul told the Ephesians, "Don't be drunk with beer or wine, but be filled with the Spirit" (Eph. 5:18, author's translation). God can't put anything in your vessel if it's already filled with something else. You've got to get rid of the earthly stuff to be filled with the Holy Spirit. If you're filled with something—anything—where will you put the Lord? If you're filled with ambition, retirement, money, plans…can God fill you? No! You must empty yourself to be filled with God.

Why did Paul instruct us not to be filled with beer and wine? To some people drinking represents fun. You can't be filled with God's Spirit if you are filled with having fun. Others drink alcohol to get away from their problems. You can't be filled with God's Spirit if you are filled with denial and anxiety. Some people get drunk because it's an addiction. But again, if you are filled with bad habits, you can't be filled with the Spirit of God. The secret of being filled with God is to first empty yourself. It's called repentance. You tell God you're sorry for breaking

His laws and promise never to do it again. Have you repented? If so, you're ready to be filled. *Lord, I repent.*

Empty yourself to drink. A woman from Sychar walked toward the well under the burning sun; it was high noon. She carried a large pot on her shoulder—it was empty. She didn't like the hot walk at midday, but there was no water in the house. She couldn't come in the cool of the morning or evening because the "respectable" women in town jeered at her, not wanting her to be seen with them.

"Give me something to drink," a voice interrupted her troubled thoughts. She didn't know that it was Jesus speaking to her; she assumed by His accent and dress that He was just another Jew.

Although she didn't know who this Man was, He knew all about her. Later she would say, "Come see a man who told me all the things I ever did." Jesus knew her marital dreams had been broken. She had sought marital bliss five times, but each expectation ended in a divorce. Jesus knew she had given up—she was empty—because now she had just moved in with a man. No wedding ceremony. No hope.

The woman who met Jesus at the well was just as empty as her pot (see Jn. 4:5-29). Her dreams were crushed, her respect gone, her future desolate. What could Jesus promise this empty woman? "Whoever drinks the water I give him will never thirst" (Jn. 4:14a NIV). But He didn't just offer her a one-time drink to satisfy her nagging craving. "The water I give him will become in

14

him a spring of water welling up to eternal life" (Jn. 4:14b NIV).

Are you empty? If not, what fills your life? Jesus says His drink will give you satisfaction. Do you need something to make you happy? If you'll empty your life of everything else, Jesus will fill it with Himself. He is water to drink. *Ah, that's good.*

When you fast to know God, don't begin seeking Him or trying to learn more about Him. Start by emptying yourself. *Lord, I surrender all to You.*

Empty a dirty and cracked vessel. Suppose you ask to be filled but it doesn't happen? Suppose you pray, "God, fill me," but you don't feel anything. Maybe there's some dirt in your glass. Emptying your vessel means more than pouring out stuff. It also means washing out the inside. The Lord cannot fill a dirty vessel. You wash a dirty glass with soap and water, then rinse it until it sparkles. Now you can fill it with milk. In the same way, you must wash your life in the blood of Christ, because "the blood of Jesus Christ...cleanseth us from all sin" (1 Jn. 1:7b).

But you say, "I don't see any sin in my life." Don't be naïve. Glasses that "look" clean to the naked eye may still contain bacteria or germs. You may have a virus that can't be seen with an outward look. You may not even know it's there. What can you do? Let the Lord search you.

Search me, O God, and know my heart: try me, and know my thoughts: and see if there be any wicked way in me, and lead me in the way everlasting (Psalm 139:23-24).

Would you pour milk in a glass with a crack or a hole? No! It would spill and be lost. Will the Lord fill you if you are rebellious or if you lie? No. He would be pouring Himself into a human vessel only to be spilt on the floor.

God will find every sin in you. He knows where the germs of sin are located, and He knows the inclinations of your heart (see Jer. 17:9-10). If you try to get God's filling but it doesn't come because there's sin (dirt or cracks) you can't see, wash or repair the glass again. You don't have to see the unseen sin, but you must cleanse it before God will fill you. Dip the glass into the liquid that will wash away all your sins-germs. Pray to God, "Cleanse me...and I will be clean; wash me, and I will be whiter than snow" (Ps. 51:7 NIV).

Emptying all types of vessels. What in you needs emptying? Think about all the different kinds of vessels. You use some vessels for cooking, such as stew pots, frying pans, and roasters. These vessels can represent your occupation, or what you do with your time. You're like cookware, filled with working or improving your talents. No matter what fills your vessel, it must be emptied before the Lord can fill it. He may change your job or allow you stay at the same vocation. When you empty yourself, you let Him make that decision.

Other people are like a bowl, platter, or decanter. These are serving vessels. Are you filled with doing things for people or your family? Even these things can take the place of Jesus. You must empty good works to be filled with God.

Others are like vessels used at a meal—a cup, glass, or soup bowl. Before the Lord will fill you with His goodness, you must empty out the husk and trash of this world.

What about flower vases, decorative pots, or planters? Some people go through life putting on a good front. They are more concerned with what people think of them than of what God thinks. You must empty your self-image and desire for respectability before He can fill you.

Finally, some people are like a popcorn bucket or beer bottle consumed at athletic events or at the movies. You must empty your pursuit of entertainment before He will fill you.

After you empty yourself, then what? Does God automatically fill you because you are empty? No. You must ask to be filled with the Lord's presence. *Lord, fill me now.*

Fasting is emptying. When you fast, obviously you stop ingesting food. What happens physically? Since you need energy to live, you survive off the food that has been stored in your body. To begin with, the food in your stomach will supply energy for about a day. Fasting will cause hunger pangs, similar to the fuel gauge in your automobile that tells you the tank is almost empty. However, unlike your car, your body doesn't stop running when it's empty. You then get energy from the stored fat in your body. So when you fast for several days, you live off your fat, which means you lose weight. That's good if you're overweight, but it can be disastrous if you're anemic.

There are certain people who are not physically able to fast. Years ago there was an extremely thin young lady working in my office. Around 3:00 in the afternoon I heard a commotion in the reception area. She had tried to fast, but had fainted. She was subsequently given some liquid to drink and bread to eat, then went home for the day and was all right. There are about 30 pathologies that prevent some from fasting; however, these people can enter the spirit of the fast while eating only necessities.

You physically empty yourself when you fast. But what about emptying yourself spiritually? When you feel hunger pangs, it should alert you to seek God all the more. "The Lord is nigh unto all them that call upon Him" (Ps. 145:18a). The longer you remain on a fast, the more you demonstrate your sincerity and desire to have His presence in your life. "The Lord is close to...all who call on Him in sincerity" (Ps. 145:18 TLB).

God will not hear you just because you stop eating. To think you'll get your prayers answered because you don't eat is legalism. But the symbolism of fasting can be very meaningful. As you allow your physical body to empty itself of food, make an intentional effort to empty your soul before God. If you honestly pray and seek Him, you can be filled. When you come empty to God—of food and self—He can fill you.

Turn to Me, says the Lord, with all your heart while there is time. Empty your hearts, not just your stomachs.

Fast with weeping and mourning. Don't just tear your clothing to impress Me, rather tear your hard hearts. Return to Me, Your Lord and God...who knows if I will give you mercy and a blessing instead of a curse? Perhaps I'll give you abundant blessings (Joel 2:12-14, author's translation).

To Take Away

You physically empty yourself when you fast. But what about emptying yourself spiritually? When you feel hunger pangs, it should alert you to seek God all the more. "The Lord is nigh unto all them that call upon Him" (Ps. 145:18). The longer you remain on a fast, the more you demonstrate your sincerity and desire to have His presence in your life. "The Lord is close to all who call on Him sincerely" (Ps. 145:18, TLB).

God will not hear you just because you quit eating. It's legalistic to think you'll get your prayers answered because you don't eat. But the symbolism can be meaningful. As you allow your physical body to empty itself of food, make an intentional effort to empty your soul before God. If you honestly pray and seek Him, you can be filled. When you come to God empty—of food *and* self—it is then that He can fill you.

Turn to me, says the Lord, with all your heart while there is time. Empty your hearts, not just your stomachs. Fast with weeping and mourning. Don't just tear your clothing to impress me, rather tear your hard hearts. Return to Me, Your Lord and God....Who knows if I will give you mercy and a blessing instead of a curse. Perhaps I'll give you abundant blessings (Joel 2:12-14, author's translation).

Chapter 2

TASTING

O taste and see that the Lord is good, blessed is every-one that enjoys intimacy with Him (Psalm 34:8, author's translation).

My wife and I have a favorite restaurant near the San Francisco airport. Actually, we like it because we enjoy a favorite waiter there. He encourages us to feel good about the food we're about to eat. "H-m-m-m good," he smiles and says when he places food in front of us. We respond the way he wants us to respond. Then he comes back with a second dish, saying, "Delicious." And when he pours more coffee, he smells the aroma and comments, "Wonderful." And of course for dessert, he beams broadly declaring, "Yum, yum." He's the best server we've ever met because he motivates us to crave the food before we place the first bite in our mouth. We like him because he inspires us to anticipate a good meal. He's like the sizzle of a good steak or the crackle of corn being popped. And to many of us, anticipation of pleasure is often more enjoyable than the pleasure itself.

When you taste the Lord, you anticipate all the good things that He is beginning to do for you. As you're fasting, you read a verse and hear God speaking to you through the words of Scripture...and then you want to hear more. You read another verse and God satisfies your hunger as you learn more about Him...and you long for more. As you read further into the Scriptures and drink of His goodness...you get thirstier. As you worship Him...you desire to praise Him more. Fasting is anticipation of meeting God, knowing He will meet with you.

You can fast for many reasons...to break addiction...for healing...to solve a continuing problem...or for revival. However, the greatest reason to fast is to get to know God and to feed on the Bread of Life. (See *Fasting for Spiritual Breakthrough* by Elmer Towns, Regal Books, for nine different fasts for nine different purposes).

Fasting
It's not about food.

How good is the taste of the Lord? When you fast, you stop eating food. But fasting is much more than just not eating. You turn away from earthly food, to feed on God. When you begin fasting, you take a mere taste of the Lord, and find out that He is good...He is very good. When you taste the Lord, you want more. *Lord, I'm hungry for You.*

While in college, I became aware of the class schedule of my future wife. So I used to place myself at strategic locations so that our paths would cross during the day. As I stood waiting for her, my heart would beat a little faster and my eyes would search in expectation. I wanted to hear her voice and talk with her. In the same way, when you put aside physical food, you begin to fast in anticipation. You want the Lord to meet with you. *Lord, I want You to feed me and satisfy me.*

Of all the foods in this world, which do you like most? I like the taste of Krispy Krème donuts, freshly baked. I call them *angel food* because they are so light they could help an angel fly. How do they taste? Like nothing else you have ever placed in your mouth. There are other things I also like to taste. I like the taste of a fresh tomato sandwich, grown in my own garden, picked early in the morning, and eaten as the sun comes up. I slice the tomato thick—one inch thick—then butter one side of the toast, with mayo on the other. Add enough salt to bring up the flavor, then I close my eyes to taste satisfaction. I taste energy and life, because I grew it in my own garden.

I like the taste of a hot, greasy hamburger…plain vanilla ice cream…warm pound cake fresh out of the oven…and a frosted mug of A&W Root Beer.

As much as I love these foods, when I fast I turn my back on it all, and I am again feeding on the Lord. "Blessed are they which do hunger and thirst after righteousness" (Mt. 5:6a). When I fast, I spend my meal times in prayer, talking to God, and in the Bible reading His

Word. But although I'm meeting with God, I know I'm not really eating the deep things of God, because I'm not that spiritual. I'm just hungering after God, merely nibbling around the edges. I am only tasting the Lord. But even then when I take a little bite, I find out...God is good! *Lord, constantly remind me how good You are.*

So when you just begin to fast, you're simply eating around the edges. Have you started to taste the things that God has provided for you? *Lord, I'm ready to get started.*

Tasting is enjoyment. When you taste food, you do not swallow a mouthful to get strength, nor do you consume as much as you can to keep from starving. No! When you taste, you put a little food on your fork, or you pinch off a piece, and place it in your mouth. Eating a full meal gives you strength; tasting is just the first step towards that strength. Tasting is the first step towards a pleasant experience.

Many people think that fasting is solely denying the body food and one obviously grows weaker because of that abstention; much like an automobile stops moving when it runs out of gas. But that's only one side of the picture. Tasting spiritual things presents a promise of more to follow. When you taste, Jesus comes to support your weakness. So when you taste the Lord, it is the first step towards spiritual strength. *Lord, I'm weak, I need You.*

When you take that first taste of the Lord, you find that He is good. Just as you enjoy conversation with your spouse, so you enjoy conversation with the Lord. And just as you look forward to fellowship with your buddies or talking to relatives at a family reunion, so you enjoy talking to the Lord when you taste of Him.

Tasting is a down payment on what is to follow. When I go to a church supper, I always enjoy potato salad. No two cooks ever make potato salad the same way. Just as there are a vast number of personalities, so there are vast tastes of potato salad. Some cooks put in a little mustard, others withhold the mustard. I personally like the taste of a little sweet relish, and a lot of hard-boiled egg whites. When I see several dishes of potato salad at a church supper, I taste a little from each bowl. Why? So I can choose which I like best and return to get a big helping of my favorite.

In the same way, fasting is like my tasting different kinds of potato salad. Enjoyment is in each anticipated bite. When you fast you begin to sample God by praying and listening to Him. After tasting His presence, you desire a big spoonful of God on your plate. Tasting the Lord is a down payment of more to follow. There is more fellowship...more enjoyment...more communion...and more union with Him.

When I came to the end of my 40-day fast, I was not famished for food. Many people who have not fasted for 40 days assume that you approach the last day like a marathon runner with barely enough strength to make it to the finish line. No! That's not the way it is. At the end of the 40 days, you want to stay on the fast...forever. You have been enjoying the presence of God, and you don't want to leave. The 40-day fast has been only a taste of what Heaven is like. You don't want to go back to the world of food again because you feel you might lose the intimate presence of God. *Lord, give me more.*

Tasting is creating desire. Usually, you taste food that you've previously enjoyed. If you haven't liked that food before, you'll pass over it the next time it is served. You taste food that you think will be good. Why? You anticipate it.

The psalmist said, "One thing have I desired of the Lord, that will I seek after; that I may dwell in the house of the Lord all the days of my life, to behold the beauty of the Lord, and to enquire in His temple" (Ps. 27:4). The great passion of David was to spend time with God, to be close to Him and enjoy His presence. That's why you fast. You know you love Him and you want more of Him in your life. Do you like the Lord? Have you tasted Him recently?

Why did David greatly desire to seek after the Lord? He explained, "For in the time of trouble He shall hide me in His pavilion: in the secret of His tabernacle shall He hide me; He shall set me up upon a rock" (Ps. 27:5). When you begin tasting of the Lord, He takes care of your problems in life. You hide in Him because you are sheltered by Him. Many of your problems evaporate because most are perceptual in nature. When you taste of God, you find that not many things in life are really worth worrying about, after all. So, set aside food, taste of the Lord; and hide yourself in His presence. If problems have been stalking you lately, seek the Lord.

A taste is an experiment. What do you do when you see some food that you're not sure you will like? You taste a little bite, not a full bite, to experiment with it. When I'm served Mexican food, I am always afraid that it includes too much Jalepeno pepper, and I don't like the taste of "hot." So if it's a Mexican dish, I sample just a little bit and hang on to my water glass in case I need to wash it down. What am I doing? I am experimenting.

You may be fasting for your first time. You're not sure what will happen to your feelings. You have felt hungry before and didn't like experiencing hunger pains, so you got something to eat. Maybe on the way home from work, you stopped for a hamburger because you felt you couldn't make it home without a little bit of food. Fasting scares you.

Then you decide to experiment. You fast for one day and you make it through that day without any problem. When you spend time with God in prayer, you find that a new spiritual hunger replaces the old physical desire.

When a boy goes to pick up a girl for a date, he doesn't stop for a hamburger on the way to her house. He's got other things on his mind. The girl is more important than food. When a young father goes to see his newborn at the hospital for the first time, he doesn't delay the visit to eat. No! When you're excited about a date, or the first sight of a baby, or anything you love; you lose your appetite for food. Likewise, you fast because you're more anxious to feed on spiritual things than to eat physical food.

When you begin experimenting with fasting, slowly you begin to lose your appetite for physical food because you are tasting the Lord. You begin to eat His goodness, and to enjoy His presence, because the first taste is a good taste. *Lord, I want more.*

Tasting activates your recessive memory. I know what to expect when I see potato salad—I anticipate pleasure. The same thing happens with certain other foods—my memory kicks in so that I enjoy it before I taste it. I love small sweet garden peas that my mother used to grow in her garden and Kentucky Wonder snap beans. When I see them, my mouth waters in anticipation because I remember how good they are. But then again, not all memories are good memories. I can pass over spinach if there are other vegetables on the table. My memory tells me that spinach is strawy, the same with broccoli, cauliflower, and asparagus. I'll eat them but I don't necessarily like or dislike them.

My taste memory sends a different alarm through my whole body at other things. My mother used to force me to take castor oil every spring and every fall. Her theory was every young boy needs a good cleaning out twice a year…kind of like changing oil in a car. So whether I was sick or not, she would pour a large tablespoonful of castor oil, grab me by the nose so I would open my mouth to breathe, and then shove it in. I hated it every time, and for days couldn't get that lingering taste of castor oil out of my memory. Just the smell of it made me gag. If she tried to get me to sip it, even a little bit, I would never let it happen. Your taste memory sends you messages about what is good, and that which is repulsive.

After you've tasted the Lord, you remember He is good, His ways are good, and when you follow Him, your life is good. So you fast to taste His presence, anticipating that He will meet you and talk with you. *Lord, forgive me for pushing You into the back room of my mind.*

Taste can be developed. When I was a small boy, I just knew I didn't like chicken noodle soup and wouldn't even taste it. I would look into the pot on the stove and see little globules of greasy chicken fat on the top of the soup, and think, Yuck! From that first perception, even the smell of chicken noodle soup was repulsive. It wasn't as bad as castor oil, but it was bad! Then one cold rainy day, Mother gave me a dime and sent me to the corner store to buy two cans of soup, a nickel a can. One can of chicken noodle soup for her, and one can of vegetable soup for me.

After the soup was warmed and served, she put a spoonful in her mouth and exclaimed, "M-m-m-m good!" I listened and thought it can't be that good. But every time she put a spoonful in her mouth, she responded, "M-m-m-m good!" Some of you may remember when Campbell Soup used the slogan, "M-m-m-m good, M-m-m-m-good." I've often thought, *They got it from my mother.*

"Wanna taste a spoonful?" she asked. And for some reason, my obstinate will that day gave in. "Okay." One taste was all it took. "This is good." My glowing eyes revealed to Mother I liked chicken noodle soup. Guess what happened? She gave me another nickel and I rode my bicycle through the rain to get my own personal can of chicken noodle soup. I developed a taste for chicken noodle soup and today I love it.

People who hate God can acquire a taste for Him. All it takes is a small taste of His goodness, and they're hooked for life. Are you hooked?

When I was president of Winnipeg Bible College, Canada, in the early 1960s, one of the board members, Mr. Hugh McKennon, the owner of a large Canadian tea company, would take me to lunch periodically to discuss the business of Winnipeg Bible College. One day while eating in a distinguished hotel, the waiter mentioned to Mr. McKennon, "We serve your brand of tea in our hotel."

Mr. McKennon smiled politely, but as soon as the waiter left he said, "This is not our tea," and he went on to explain what country the tea came from, and how many thousands of feet in elevation the tea grew. He was a tea taster who could distinguish the kind of tea, the country where it was grown, and its elevation.

Wow, I thought this was an extraordinary ability. Then he shocked me by saying, "I can teach you to be a tea taster..."

He continued to discuss how I could acquire the taste to become a tea taster, but I never took him up on his offer. I was busy in the Lord's work and wanted to give myself fully to ministry. Even so, he claimed I could have acquired the skill of tea tasting. If you can acquire a physical ability to determine the differences between teas, why can't you acquire the ability to determine the differences in your spiritual taste for God? *O God, help me learn to know when I am tasting Your best.*

Your taste can be hidden or covered. When you drink scalding coffee or bite a mouthful of crushed ice, you suddenly lose your ability to taste anything. Immediately after burning or freezing your mouth, it's as though your taste buds bail out so that you don't recognize anything in your mouth. The food is neither good nor bad; you don't know what it is because you've destroyed your taste buds.

In the same manner, when you put sin in your mouth, what happens to your taste for God? Like boiling hot water, you scald the inside of your mouth so that you taste nothing. You might even compare the more vile sin to the hottest boiling water. And of course you know the hotter the water, the more damage it does to your mouth. Have you damaged your spiritual taste buds? *O God, grow a new appetite in my heart to love and serve You more.*

There is no taste for something you've never tried. Sometimes you're puzzled when you look at certain foods on your plate. Your taste buds don't kick in because you've never seen this food before. Nothing happens. There is no recessive memory to which your taste can relate. You don't know if what's on your plate is good or vile because you have never tasted it.

Some people have no desire to fast because they've never tried it. They think giving themselves to God is the worst choice they could make because they will have to give up their friends, their drinks, their fleshly activities, and their sinful amusements. These people are not ready to make the trade to give up the world for Jesus Christ. Just as you're not aware of the taste of food that you've never tried, they don't know how satisfying Jesus Christ can be. Are you afraid to give all to Jesus Christ? Then give up food, fast to know Him better. *Lord, I will fast to know You.*

Taste is a trigger. What is a trigger? Something that sets off a reaction or a chain of events. The trigger of a gun sets off an explosion, and the trigger to a trap leads to a capture.

Your taste can trigger physical reactions in your body. As soon as I take a taste of watermelon to find out that it's sweet and juicy, my mouth waters for more.

Sometimes taste will make us hungrier than we think we are. Other times, a repulsive taste can make us gag or even actually throw up. Even if we're actually hungry, we lose our appetite to eat.

Taste also triggers mental pictures or associational connections. When I taste stuffed baked pork chops, I remember the way my mother-in-law, Mrs. E.B. Forbes cooked them. And when I taste stuffed bell peppers, I remember the way Mrs. Lawrence Schultz in Winnipeg, Canada, prepared them. Meatloaf causes me to think of the Cracker Barrel Restaurant and egg custard makes me remember my mother's favorite dessert.

When you taste the Lord, it triggers various reactions in your heart. Sometimes, when you fast, God lays it upon your heart to intercede for a lost relative. Other times, fasting triggers your desire to study the Word, and still at other times, fasting triggers your desire to worship, praise, and magnify the Lord. Sometimes, you will remember a sermon that you heard, and again apply the message to your heart. At other times, a person will pop into your mind as you fast, so you'll pray for that person.

One of the greatest associational triggers that occur when I fast is Bible insight. As I am fasting and studying the Word, I see lessons in Scripture that I have never thought about before. God reveals to me meanings from the Bible with new applications for my life. *Lord, use my fasting to know You better.*

To Take Away

When God created people, He gave them the ability to taste. It protected them or helped them stay away from poisonous or harmful food. But it also gave people enjoyment in life. Isn't God good to give us enjoyment from something so simple as putting fuel in our bodies to strengthen us and help us to function? Eating could have been as perfunctory as pouring gasoline into the tank of a car. It would have met a basic need but given us very little physical pleasure. However, God gave us the wonderful ability to taste foods like ice cream. Isn't He a wonderful Creator? Why don't you stop now to thank Him.

Maybe God gave us the ability to taste so we could ultimately understand what it means to enjoy Him...not to be scared of Him, or to simply obey Him, or study Him; but so that we would anticipate Him, and understand Him. And just as we enjoy food, we would enjoy Him. *Ah, it's good to rest in You.*

If you like God, why don't you tell Him now!

TASTING

NOTES

Chapter 3

WAITING

Rest in the Lord, and wait patiently for Him (Psalm 37:7).

Truly my soul waiteth upon God: from Him cometh my salvation (Psalm 62:1).

Therefore will the Lord wait, that He may be gracious unto you...blessed are all they that wait for Him (Isaiah 30:18).

Most Christians today have lost the virtue of waiting. We have instant food, instant access computers, instant banking, instant everything. Our cell phones allow us to reach anybody from anywhere immediately. We seldom have to wait. We can fly across the continent or around the world, quickly. I left Virginia on a Monday, spoke in Thailand on Tuesday, Wednesday, and Thursday, and was back in my classes in Lynchburg, Virginia, on Friday. In a world that says hurry...now...immediate...

urgent...bottom line; what can the art of waiting teach us? We can learn the goodness of God. "The Lord is good unto them that wait for Him" (Lam. 3:25). *Lord, here I am.*

We all know that God is good because we've heard it said many times. Children are taught at a young age to pray before meals, "God is great, God is good..." But a lot of people don't know how good God is because they've not actually experienced the goodness of God. Perhaps you don't think that God is good. Maybe it's because you haven't been waiting on Him.

Waiting is a school. You can learn many things while you are waiting. For example, you can study human nature by stopping to watch people go by. The great thing about waiting is that you see many things you would have missed if you had not been waiting. When you wait on God, you will discover many things you've never known before. Fasting is an excellent time to wait on God to experience His goodness. Those who continue to wait before God will learn, "The Lord is good unto them that wait for Him." Waiting is also a time to learn about worship, adoring, and trusting. Waiting is a school where we can learn about God Himself.

What do you want when you wait on God? Most of us wait for God because we want Him to give us something. Like children waiting for Christmas, we are anxious to know what's in the packages. Will we get a toy to entertain us? Or will we get clothes to warm us? Maybe we'll get perfume to make us smell good, or candy to stuff us. When you wait for God, are you waiting for His gifts? Or, are you waiting for Him? *Lord, teach me to wait on You.*

Have you thought why God may withhold His gifts from you? Maybe you've not been serious when you wait on God, like a child who fusses and pitches a temper tantrum waiting for Christmas. The impatient child doesn't understand the mystery of Christmas, nor does he enter into the proper spirit of waiting. God may not answer your prayers immediately because you are more interested in His gifts than you are in God Himself. However, the more you fast, the more serious you become about God. And when you have fasted two or three days, you reveal that you're changing from a restless, irritable child to one who is deeply interested in and earnestly seeking God.

Waiting binds you to the gift and the giver. Yes, waiting makes you focus on the contents of a package, but waiting also teaches you to think about the giver. It binds you to the one who gives the gifts. Therefore, as you quietly wait on God, think of entering into His goodness, think of entering into His presence. Then, the exercise of waiting becomes attractive to you because you get something for waiting. You get God. *Lord, bind my heart on You.*

The expectancy of waiting. Is there a purpose to your waiting? When you wait on God, are you waiting for Him to do something or are you waiting to tell Him something? Or is it best when to just wait for God Himself?

When a young man goes on a date with his sweetheart, most of the time he doesn't care where they eat or what they do, he just wants to be with her. In the same way, she doesn't care where they go, she just wants to be with him. The greatest thing about waiting is expectancy. What do you expect when you wait on God? *Lord, I expect to know You better.*

"Therefore I will look unto the Lord; I will wait for the God of my salvation: my God will hear me" (Mic. 7:7). What does it mean to expect something? It means you are on the lookout, you focus your ears to listen, and you train your eyes to see. Expectancy is to anticipate something. You hold your breath, you prepare, you hope. Isn't *hope* a good word? Growing your hope is the very essence of waiting on God. When you hope in God, it means you believe God will help you and will one day return for you. You know that God is the One who "calls the things that are not as though they were" (see Rom. 4:17). When you expectantly wait on Him, it builds up both hope and faith. You should enjoy waiting on God because your faith grows while waiting. *Lord, I want You.*

The art of waiting. You can learn how to wait. It's an art. Consider children waiting for Christmas Day. Some of them sneak to check the packages. Others try to pry the answer out of a parent. Still others fidget…squirm…and some can't sleep at night.

What parent would give into his children by letting them open their gifts on December 12? That's not the way it's done. If you open your gifts early, you destroy the whole nature of Christmas. Waiting is an art, and children must learn the art of waiting until Christmas Day to get their gifts.

In the same way, waiting on God is an art that can be discovered and perfected. Do you have trouble finding time to wait on God? That's quite normal, for the natural person is a self-centered person, fulfilling selfish needs. Christianity is intentional; you must choose God and deny yourself (see Lk. 9:23). Spirituality is intentional; you must decide to seek God and sacrifice selfish pursuits. So decide now to wait on God. *Lord, make me wait on You.*

Why should you wait in God's presence? When you learn the secret art of waiting, you will find the heart of God. Someone has said we become holy when we learn to wait, because we become like God. "...The Lord wait[s] that He may be gracious unto you" (Is. 30:18). Waiting is a quality of God. We become like Him when we learn to wait. *Lord, I want to be like You.*

Think about the farmer. He plants the seeds, then waits for the harvest. There is not much he can do to speed up growth from seed to harvest time. The Bible describes the farmer: "...waiting for the precious fruit of the earth, and has long patience for it" (Jas. 5:7, author's translation). Just as you cannot gather fruit until it is ripe, so there are prayers that God doesn't answer until He is ready. So what must you do? *Lord, teach me to wait.*

And for what do you wait? Like the farmer, you are waiting for the sunshine of God's love to give life; you're waiting for the rain of God's blessing to give life; and you're *waiting* for the seed to reach full fruit.

Timing is everything. When we talk about *waiting,* we're implying waiting for the right time. Sometimes God waits to answer your prayers, because now is not the right time. Maybe you need to learn more lessons. Maybe circumstances need to change. When you pray for a friend or relative to get saved, it may take time for God to bring someone into that person's life who will share the gospel, or it may take time for that person to be convicted of their sins. Timing is everything with God.

If God could wait 4,000 years until the fullness of time to send His Son into the world, surely He's not going to hurry for you. Remember, you can't hurry God like some of us try to hurry a slow waiter in a restaurant or hurry a child who is grudgingly getting ready for school. *My times are in Your hands.*

As you are waiting, remember that while God prepares to give you something, He will do it on His timetable, not yours. God wants us to learn the lesson that He is everything. So, the next time you are waiting on God, remember that right around the corner may be the greatest thing you've ever received in life. It may be that God Himself will be there. *Lord, I'm waiting.*

There are even more benefits you receive from waiting. Maybe you've lost your strength in your recent dash to get where you're at. You've been running through life, running to work, running to home, and running to church. Now, you need to take time to fast. Why? "They that wait upon the Lord shall renew their strength" (Is. 40:31a). What happens when you wait? You catch your breath, your muscles rest, and your pulse returns to normal. Waiting on God renews your spiritual strength. Are you drained? Then pray and wait on God while you fast. It will renew your strength.

Notice some other things that happen when you wait on God: "But they that wait upon the Lord shall renew their strength; they shall mount up with wings as eagles; they shall run, and not be weary; and they shall walk, and not faint" (Is. 40:31). Wait on God and you will mount up...walk...run...and not faint. Is that what you need to do? Then fast, and wait. *Okay, Lord, I'm here.*

"For since the beginning of the world men have not heard, nor perceived by the ear, neither hath the eye seen, O God, beside Thee, what He hath prepared for him that waiteth for Him" (Is. 64:4).

If you looked in a mirror, what would you see yourself doing as you wait upon God? Are you nervously tapping your fingers? Or, are you quietly waiting for Him? The best way to wait on God is...quietly. "It is good that a man should...quietly wait for the salvation of the Lord." (Lam. 3:26). *Lord, I'm quiet.*

Waiting quietly. When you fast, your physical system slows down as you take a break from your normal life. The best way to do that is to wait quietly. "In quietness and in confidence shall be your strength..." (Is. 30:15b).

I believe there is a close connection between quietness and faith. I have real questions about those who pray loudly, demandingly, and brazenly. "It is good that a man should...quietly wait" (Lam. 3:26). Why? "The Lord is in

His holy temple: let all the earth keep silence before Him" (Hab. 2:20).

What does *quiet* mean? It's hard to fellowship with God in a noisy restaurant; likewise, it's difficult to have your quiet time on a busy airplane or a commuter train. This does not mean that you cannot meditate on God or pray when people are around. You can talk to God at any place. You can quiet your spirit anywhere. *Lord, teach me silence.*

When you fast, find a quiet place where you can wait on God alone. A quiet place to meditate, pray, and read Scripture, a quiet place where you won't be interrupted. In the stillness of your room, separate yourself from the world and your family, then shut yourself up to God, alone. Let the Word of God and prayer become very precious to you. Get still so you can hear the voice of God speaking to you. Then, wait quietly before God; don't even read the Bible, nor try to talk to Him. It's possible that sometimes even reading, praying, and other spiritual activities can get in the way of God Himself.

When God says, "Be still, and know that I am God" (Ps. 46:10a), He wants you to be quiet, be still, and learn something as you wait.

Consider that there is no stillness like the grave. There is a special silence when you walk through the graveyard and read the tombstones. Being there you feel close to nature, perhaps because the area is so well manicured. It should also make us feel close to God because visiting a cemetery reminds us that in death we are closer to God than any other time of life. Believers buried in a cemetery are as close to God as they can get.

So when you wait on God, you build up your hope that the Lord will come back for you. When you become still before God, you learn to die daily to the cares of this world. When you fast in His presence, you temporarily put to death the appetites of the body, which is symbolic of putting to death the appetites of sinful lust. As you cease feeding your body, your soul becomes filled with God. This is when you learn the lesson, "Be still and know that I am God" (Ps. 46:10a).

Think of the disciples in the howling storm. Think of the disciples fighting the threatening waves...blowing wind...yelling...facing death. Then suddenly Jesus appears and says, "Peace, be still" (Mk. 4:39b). Instantly, not a splashing wave was felt, not a whistling wind was heard. Silence...stillness...quietness...that's what happens when you wait before Jesus, your Savior. *Lord, I feel peaceful in Your presence.*

What does God do while you wait? "Therefore will the Lord wait, that He may be gracious unto you...blessed are all they that wait for Him" (Is. 30:18). God waits for us as we wait for Him. Why? He is waiting for us to recognize Him, love Him, and worship Him. He's waiting for us to come to Him with the right attitude and for the right reasons. *Lord, I'm slowing down.*

Have you ever thought that God may wait longer than you expect, maybe because He wants to give you twice as much as you expect? Sometimes you get anxious when you wait. Maybe you don't like the way God is directing your life, and you don't like the way things are unfolding. You impatiently pray like Isaiah, "Oh that Thou wouldest rend the heavens, that Thou wouldest come down" (Is. 64:1a). You want God to ride in on a white horse and kill all the bad men. You want God to split Heaven to reveal Himself to you. If He can't do that, then you want Him to instantly make you a millionaire, like participating on a popular television game show. Notice what Isaiah wanted God to do: "When Thou didst terrible things which we looked not for, Thou camest down, the mountains flowed down at Thy presence" (Is. 64:3). You, like Isaiah, would like God to flow down the mountains to straighten things out.

You need to know that the God you are complaining about is the same God who sent the ten terrible plagues on Pharaoh in Egypt. He was waiting for the right time to deliver His people. He is also the same God who waited patiently for 400 years between the Old and New Testament. Not a sound was heard out of Heaven in those 400 years. Why? God was waiting for the right time to send His Son to earth. Maybe God is waiting for the right time to do something in your life? *Lord, teach me patience.*

Maybe you think you can get God to answer sooner if you shout louder. Maybe you think you can get God to jump if you pray longer. Maybe you think the solution is to get the whole church to fast and pray. God is still the same God today as He was during Bible times. He hasn't changed His nature, and He hasn't changed the way He does things. God alone knows what He can do by waiting, and God knows what He can do by getting you to wait. So, why don't you fast...slow down...and wait on God?

The fact that God is waiting on you is an unspeakable blessing that ought to motivate you to the highest form of worship. The God of the universe is waiting on you.

To Take Away

Why is it that most of us hate to wait for service, for events, for people, for anything...? That's an interesting question. When you answer it, you've analyzed why most people don't wait on God.

Maybe people don't like to wait because they're an "on-time person." They've been trained to never be late for anything. Because they never run not late, they dislike anyone or anything that's late. Is that why you don't like to wait on God? If so, analyze yourself. When you don't wait on God, you're saying your habits are more important than God. You don't want to interrupt your way of doing things—being on time—to actually wait on God. Surrender your habits to God and wait on Him.

Maybe people don't like to wait because "time is money." They think valuable time and money are wasted when waiting on God. But what about sacrifice? Aren't Christians supposed to put "Jesus First"? Aren't Christians supposed to surrender everything to God? If you've yielded everything to Him, then run your life by His timetable. Wait on God.

Still other people don't like to wait because they are activity driven. They get bored just waiting around. But think again. Waiting is not just a zero...a stop...a nothing. Waiting is active; it involves every part of your being— your mind, emotions, and the decision to do it. When you're waiting, you're learning God...growing in Christ... becoming transformed.

There are others who hate to wait because they're selfish. They think the world revolves around them and refuse to inconvenience themselves for others. Ah! This person needs to understand that the essence of Christianity is putting Christ first. "For to me to live is Christ" (Phil. 1:21a). When Jesus becomes the passion of your life, you want to wait on Him. So if Jesus has control of your life, *wait on Him.*

NOTES

Waiting

Chapter 4

COMING

Come unto Me, all ye that labour and are heavy laden, and I will give you rest. Take My yoke upon you, and learn of Me; for I am meek and lowly in heart: and ye shall find rest unto your souls (Matthew 11:28-29).

A s a young boy I remember playing till suppertime, then I'd hear my mother call, "El...mer..." Since not many boys were named *Elmer*, I knew it meant me. I usually dropped what I was doing to run home.

Even at times when my mother didn't use my name, I never confused her voice with the voices of other mothers calling their sons. While I couldn't always distinguish the voices of other older women, I always knew my own mother's voice. I had grown up obeying it. I could tell when she was angry and about to punish me. I also could tell when she had something good waiting for me. The suppertime call was a good call, so I usually dropped what I was doing to go home.

If I happened not to respond immediately, her *good call* to supper became her *irritated call.* Then I quickly obeyed before it became an *angry call.*

There were several reasons why I usually answered her call immediately: partially training—she taught me to come; partly fear—I didn't want a spanking; partially love—I wanted to please my mother. But mostly it was hunger. I obeyed the supper call for food. My mother was the best cook in the neighborhood. At lunchtime all the guys played around my house because they loved my mother's cooking and she loved to feed boys.

But suppertime meant every boy went home to eat. That's what I did. When mother called, I went home to eat.

This chapter is about answering the call of the Lord. How do you respond when the Lord calls you? Do you come immediately, or must He call several times before you make a move? Do you come because of fear...or because of love...or because of training? Or do you come when He calls because you want to eat at His table? Do you enjoy God's food?

Fasting is not so much about leaving earthly food as it is about coming to the Lord's Table to enjoy His fellowship, to eat His food, to know Him intimately. *Lord, I'm hungry.*

Most people begin fasting by focusing on what they won't do—won't eat, won't enjoy food, won't go to a restaurant. However, fasting shouldn't be a *negation*. Not eating is just dieting. Rather, fasting is an *affirmation*—what you will do. So what do you do positively when you fast?

Fasting is coming to Jesus. When you fast, you come to the Lord Jesus, leaving behind the natural world with its requirements of food, enjoyment, physical repletion, and restoration of energy. Jesus is calling you to Himself. When you fast, you have obeyed the call of Jesus and you come to Him. *Lord, here I come.*

Jesus expects you to come. Sometimes people say, "Come over to our house sometime," or "Drop over sometime." It's a nice way to end a conversation, but they don't really expect you to come. Jesus, however, is different. When He invites you to "come," He truly looks forward to your arrival, and when you get there, He will welcome you. Jesus is glad when you come to Him.

Will you be disappointed when you come to Jesus? There are many people in the world who are disappointed about Jesus Christ. Some have never really come to Him because of the faulty information they have heard about Jesus Christ. They have never actually come to Him based on the principles of the Bible. They've been frustrated by their trials, sufferings, or even their failure to avoid temptation. Why are some people disappointed in Jesus? They've probably never fully understood the word *come.*

Some people only come halfway to Jesus, but in this way they will never experience holding Him intimately. And, of course, who isn't disappointed in a hug when the other person doesn't hug back? Others come to Jesus while clutching their prized possessions behind their back. They will not give everything to Jesus; as a result, they too are disappointed because He cannot bless them or use them. Jesus won't bless the things we withhold from Him.

Then again, there are others who walk backwards into His presence, not looking into His face, nor enjoying His fellowship. They have something to hide, so these too are disappointed in Jesus.

Next, some people answer Jesus' invitation to "come" but rush right pass Him, instead of approaching Him. Why? Maybe they look for other pleasures in life, or the next thrilling weekend. However, you will never be satisfied with Jesus unless you come to Him and wait in His presence. To be completely satisfied with Jesus Christ means you fully understand the word *come*, you sincerely acted upon it, and you obeyed it exactly as He commanded. When He said "come," you *came*.

Still there are other people who are disappointed because they come for something other than Him. Some come for music—they enjoy singing. Some come for academic stimulation—lessons in the Bible. And others come out of habit. Do you remember the last time you entered the presence of Jesus? What did you experience, and how did you feel? Were you glad that you came to Jesus and did He keep His word? Will He receive you with open arms this time? *Lord, I know You'll receive me.* When you honestly come to Jesus, you will never be disappointed with Him. As a matter of fact, there is nothing fuller than coming to Jesus, there is nothing richer than that encounter. There is nothing in the world like meeting Jesus Christ. Why do you come to Jesus? *I come to You, Lord, because I love You.*

Have you ever wondered why Jesus invites you to **come**? It's hard to believe that Jesus is serious about the invitation. Why does He ask you to come to Him? What can you do for Him that He can't do for Himself? Nothing. Are you good enough to come to Him or fellowship with Him? No. "All have sinned" (Rom. 3:23a). "All we like sheep have gone astray" (Is. 53:6a). So why would He call you? The only explanation is because of something inside Himself—His principle of grace. He gives you the exact opposite of what you deserve. You deserve punishment for your disobedience, but He gives you His presence. Why? Jesus gives you what He desires for you to have. He loves us even while we are unlovely. *Lord, I want all You have for me.*

What happens when you come to Jesus? He will open His arms to you. Have you ever been hugged by Jesus? Then He will open His heart to you. Have you ever been loved by Jesus? Then He opens His life and strength to you. Have you ever been empowered by Jesus? When Jesus says, "Come," He opens His presence. There you will experience the meaning of life that you will not encounter anywhere else. *Lord, I come to know You.*

Why do people actually come? Some come because they are lonely and want fellowship with God. Is that why you come? Some come because they are lost and searching for God. When they hear His invitation to *come*, they respond. Others are suffering under sin—it's such a cruel taskmaster—so it is easy for them to repent and come to Jesus. He is a loving Master. Others come because of Jesus' self-sacrifice on the cross. What else could they do but come to Him because He died for them? Still others come because they are addicted in miserable bondage to sin whether drugs, alcohol, or sex. When Jesus says, "Come," His word is the release of freedom to break through their slavery. Finally, there are some who come because they want to go to Heaven. They want to spend eternity in the presence of God. So when Jesus says, "Come," they come to Him for eternal life.

Have you fully come into His presence? When Jesus invites you to come, do you stand in the doorway? Some come to Jesus, but they won't go all the way into the house—they stand outside the door. Still others enter, bur remain in the front hall. What good is it to obey the King's invitation, but not go all the way into the King's presence? When Jesus invites you to *come* it isn't to enter the basement, nor is it to go to a shack in the backyard. He says, "Come unto Me." He wants you to come all the way into His presence. Have you been there lately? Obey His invitation and enter the full life that He offers.

When Jesus says, "*Come*," He means for you to come to Him in the daytime...in the nighttime...all the time. When Jesus say, "*Come*," He requires a total commitment of your time. Just as you can't enter a house and leave part of yourself outside at the same time, you can't come to Jesus and leave part of your life outside. He will enable you to come and give you the strength to do it. He wants all of your life. *Lord, here I come.*

How should you come to Jesus? When you come to Jesus, you must come humbly and expectantly like Mary, who "also sat at Jesus' feet, and heard His word" (Lk. 10:39b). Why don't you sit down at the feet of Jesus, look up into His loving eyes, and wait for Him to speak to you? Like Mary who sat at His feet to learn from Him, you need to listen to His holy voice. Jesus has something to say to you and you need to hear it now.

The promise of rest. When Jesus says, "Come, he twice repeats the promise of rest. First, He says, "*Come* unto Me, I will give you rest." This is the rest of *salvation.* Second he says, "Take My yoke upon you and learn of Me and ye shall *find* rest." This is the rest of *victory over sin.*

When you first come to Jesus you immediately receive rest—instant forgiveness of sin with immediate peace that comes from salvation. This first rest is pardon. You rest in Him because you have been forgiven.

"Ye shall find rest" is the second rest. This is a rest you must look for and find. While Jesus gives the first rest, you must *do something* to gain the second rest. This second rest is acquired when you learn how to overcome daily temptation. Not all of God's children have this second rest because it is something you must attain. It is found only upon entire surrender and commitment to Jesus Christ. *Lord, I surrender all.*

Many people come to the first *rest* in salvation. God forgives their sins, gives them eternal life, and they begin walking with Jesus Christ. But they are not careful about the ongoing influence of sin. Rather than being horrified at the thought of disobeying God, they find the beauty of temptation attractive. Before they know it, they no longer enjoy the second rest in Jesus' victory over sin. Why? They are sinning. What must they do to find that rest again? Jesus says, "Take My yoke, and learn of Me." You must do two things: You must *take* and you must *learn*. These are the conditions of discipleship, and when you become a disciple you find the second *rest*.

The second rest is not something that you can attain apart from Jesus. Even though some try to experience rest by other means, they will never be fulfilled until they search for Jesus. When you get Jesus and Jesus gets you, you find rest. What do you really want in life? Rest! Who gives it to you? Jesus!

Many young believers have not laid hold of this truth about the second *rest*, and so they continue to live defeated lives. They don't understand that the Christian life is wrestling...running...battling...and getting victory in Jesus, in order to enjoy His peace. Their life is spiritually useless. The longer you stay in a useless condition, the more you get used to it, and soon, much of your life has passed away.

When Jesus says, "Come," is it a command or an invitation? Is He commanding you to come to Him, as an army officer might use His authority to command a recruit? Or is His an invitation of love because He knows you are tired and needy? Both are true. When you are tired of sin, He kindly invites you to come for forgiveness. At the same time, He is a military officer who commands you as a disciple to *come* and be trained for service and battle.

The Word of God has been described as a "small voice" but yet His voice can be mightier than the storm that breaks rocks into pieces. His Word is the hammer that crushes the hardest of hearts. But when you hear Him say *come*, it's not an angry voice, but a gentle command. It is Jesus saying, "Abide in Me." *Lord, I'm comfortable.*

When the Lord says, "Come," how close can you can get to Him? His invitation to *come* offers you the unique closeness that only a child can have with his father. His word *come* offers you the intimacy of fellowship with Him that the world doesn't understand. The word *come* also includes knowing the wonders of life and the purpose you can have in Jesus Christ.

When you surrender yourself to Jesus and *come* to Him, you will not be concerned with the loss of your life, or the abandoning of your ambitions. For you have everything to gain. You are acquiring an unspeakable privilege of knowing Jesus Christ and intimately abiding in Him. *Lord, I'm taking my first step to You.*

To Take Away

When I played ball as a young boy, two of the bigger guys would pick their teams from all the smaller guys who came to play. I was usually among the last chosen because I was one of the smallest.

When one of the big guys finally pointed to me and said, "Come over here," adrenaline shot through my system. I jumped...I yelled...and I smiled a lot. I slapped hands with my teammates; it was warming to be included on the team. It's a wonderful feeling to be chosen; it's comforting to hear the invitation, "Come."

Because I was honored by the captain's choice, I determined to do my very best, to give my team 100 percent effort. I was so glad to be called. I never complained about being called last, nor did I ever give a halfhearted effort because I wasn't called first. As a matter of fact, I was so delighted with being called, that I determined to work harder than anyone else on the team. Even though I wasn't the largest boy, the most talented, or the first called, I gave it my best every time, all the time. Should we do less for God who calls us? Never hang back. Get on the team as fast as you can. "Faithful is He that calleth you, who also will do it" (1 Thess. 5:24).

NOTES

Chapter 5

DRINKING

But whosoever drinketh of the water that I shall give him shall never thirst; but the water that I shall give him shall be in him a well of water springing up into everlasting life (John 4:14).

He that believeth on Me shall never thirst (John 6:35b).

When Jesus went through Samaria, a country racially different from His Jewish heritage, He stopped at a well, tired and famished. The original language suggests He slumped into a seat, completely exhausted. The disciples had traveled on into town to buy "hamburgers." While they were gone, a woman came at noonday to draw water from the well, which was contrary to the other women who came either in the cool of the morning or the evening. Jesus said to her, "Give Me some water to drink."

The woman was surprised at His request for two reasons. First, a man would not speak to a woman; and second, a Jew would never associate with a Samaritan. When the woman of Samaria questioned why Jesus, a Jew, would ask a drink from her, He answered, "If you knew the gift of God, and who it is who says to you, 'Give Me a drink,' you would have asked Him, and He would have given you living water" (Jn. 4:10 NKJV). In His answer, Jesus used water to suggest his offer of spiritual satisfaction. Just as a person needs to drink physical water in order to live, so must he drink living water of Jesus in order to gain eternal life. Just as a person enjoys a cool drink of water when he is tired or thirsty, so can he enjoy the satisfaction of everlasting water that Jesus offers to the weary soul.

The woman protested, saying that Jesus didn't have a bucket or rope, and that the well was deep. She was still thinking about physical water. Jesus continued to explain spiritual satisfaction, "But whosoever drinketh of the water that I shall give him shall never thirst; but the water that I shall give him shall be in him a well of water springing up into everlasting life" (Jn. 4:14). In His answer, Jesus suggested that those who drink from Him will (1) never thirst again, and (2) will have a well springing up in them from which they and others could drink.

Fasting is drinking from God's presence. There are two basic types of fasts: First, there is the absolute fast when you don't eat any solid foods or drink any liquids; the second is a normal fast, where you do not eat any solid foods, but drink water, juices, or other liquids. When you are fasting to God, you put away solid foods to eat of Jesus who is the Bread of Life. In your normal fast you may drink water or juice, but make sure that your primary passion is to drink from the Eternal Well of Salvation. To know God passionately, you must drink of Him when you seek Him through fasting. *Drinking* can direct you to the presence of God.

Drinking for enjoyment and satisfaction. When the woman came to the well to get natural water, Jesus told her He could give her "living water." She thought He was offering some kind of magical water so she'd never thirst again and never have to come to the well again. She was searching for physical satisfaction. The woman had been married five times and was presently living with a man who was not her husband. She was still searching for the perfect mate and still had not found happiness in marriage. Jesus told her that she could find ultimate satisfaction in Him. Have you come to Jesus and are you perfectly satisfied with Him?

The most wonderful thing about fasting is that you set aside food so you can focus on being completely satisfied with Jesus Christ. Then you can say with Paul, "For to me to live is Christ, and to die is gain" (Phil. 1:21). Paul's greatest passion was Jesus Christ. "That I may know Him, and the power of His resurrection, and the fellowship of His sufferings, being made conformable unto His death" (Phil. 3:10). When you fast, you learn to enjoy Jesus Christ, and you want to become like Him. *Lord, I want to be satisfied with You.*

Drinking to quench your thirst. When I was a boy, I went camping with a group on Causten Bluff, one of the sea islands off the Georgia coast. We were able to walk out to the island at low tide, but when the tide came in, we were stranded on the island. We had brought our boy scout camping gear and planned to cook an evening meal and breakfast the next morning. That night around the campfire, we got a hankering for hot chocolate. We had seen our mothers mix chocolate with water to make cocoa, so we did the same thing. We poured Hershey's Chocolate into water and brought it to a boil over an open fire. But when we tried to drink it, the bitter taste turned our mouths inside out. We didn't realize that we also needed powdered milk and sugar to make cocoa.

Then we discovered that we had made a really terrible mistake—we mixed all our water with chocolate so that the only water we had left to drink was bitter. There was no fresh water on the island, and we couldn't get to the mainland at high tide. Fortunately, we hadn't made a second mistake by throwing the bitter chocolate water away. I was thirsty the next morning and tried a little bit of the cocoa water, but spat it out. As the morning stretched on, and the sun grew hotter, it seemed liked the tide took forever to go out. Before we were able to leave the island, we were willing to drink bitter chocolate water because we were so thirsty.

Have you ever been thirsty, so thirsty you would drink dirty water from a mud puddle? Probably not. To do that, you would have to be extremely thirsty. What about spiritually thirsty? Have you ever been so spiritually thirsty for God that you couldn't stand it? Have you said, "I must have a drink of water from Jesus Christ because only He satisfies"? When everything in your life tastes like bitter chocolate water, drink the refreshing water given by Jesus Christ. *Lord, You are refreshing.*

Drinking for strength. One of the reasons you drink water is for physical strength. When you fast for God, you may lose a little physical strength, but you gain spiritual strength. As a high school boy I used to race bicycles 20 and 50 miles in a day. To give me strength, Mother would make a large milkshake of milk, raw eggs, vanilla, and sugar for me to drink. It was quite enjoyable. With five or six raw eggs and almost a quart of milk in me, I had enough strength to race 20 miles at breakneck speed without stopping.

When you drink of Jesus Christ, He gives you spiritual strength to make it through the troubles of the day. When you give up earthly food and drink of Jesus Christ, you get spiritual strength. It's then you learn, "I can do all things through Christ which strengtheneth me" (Phil. 4:13).

What happens when you don't get enough water? Sometimes your head gets light, or dizzy; sometimes you faint. Maybe you used to follow Jesus, but somewhere along the road you fainted. You stopped following Jesus. Now, you need a drink of water from Jesus. Drink! He will renew your strength to start living the Christian life again.

Drinking to keep from dying. Only a few are able to go more than two or three days without water. However, their physical pain becomes so daunting that they're unable to pray with a clear mind or a focused spirit. You should not try an absolute fast for more than three days. You will dehydrate, your digestive system will stop functioning properly, and lack of water in your system will cause permanent damage to the membranes of your brain. While some may endure a few more than seven days without water, they permanently harm their body. So, be very careful when you fast without water. *Lord, just as natural water gives me life, give me Your well of water that springs up into everlasting life.*

Drinking moistens your mouth so you can talk. Sometimes you can't talk properly because your mouth feels like cotton. A dry mouth makes it difficult to say anything. What about spiritually? With a dry mouth you have difficulty praying to God. What must you do? You must drink from Jesus Christ so your mouth is refreshed to pray. *Lord, refresh me.*

Jonathan Edwards had written a sermon that he felt would make an impact upon his church. He promised God that he would keep an absolute fast (no water) for three days before preaching the sermon. He spent His time praying for God's power upon the sermon. At approximately four o'clock on Sunday afternoon, two hours from ending his fast, Jonathan Edwards began to choke and gag. He knew he couldn't preach, and he felt he would die from choking. So he violated his fast and drank water. That night he was a broken man as he ascended the steps to the pulpit. He was devastated in his lack of self-discipline to carry the fast through until sundown. Holding a kerosene lamp in one hand and the sermon in the other, he read *Sinners in the Hand of an Angry God.* And the Spirit of God poured forth on his listeners, so much so, that they grabbed the post of the church, thinking they were slipping into hell. That sermon began the First Great Awakening and revival swept through the 13 colonies. It wasn't the fast that God had used, God anointed the *brokenness* of Jonathan Edwards so that one sermon touched Colonial America. *Lord, what will it take to break me?*

When you fast, you come to Jesus Christ to drink of Him. He gives you the ability to pray to Him, as well as the power to speak for Him. Have you been praying lately but can't get through? Try refreshing your mouth by drinking of Him—fast.

> *If any man thirst, let him come unto Me, and drink.*
> *He that believeth on Me, as the scripture hath said,*
> *out of his belly shall flow rivers of living water* (John
> 7:37b-38).

How can you drink of Him? In the exhortation above, Jesus first tells you to come to Him. Are you thirsty? Then come to Jesus Christ. How do you do that? You come to Him through prayer, simply by bowing your head and talking to Him. You come to Him by listening to His Word. You do that by reading what He tells you in the Bible. You come to Him by confessing so He can restore fellowship with you and you can enter into His presence. If you are far away, why don't you take a first step to Him now? *Lord, here I come.*

The second exhortation in this Scripture from Jesus is to *drink*. You don't need to be told how to drink. First, you see a cup of water and you know you want it. Then you reach out for it with your hand. Next, you lift the cup to your lips and tilt it so that the water flows down into your mouth. Then, you swallow and enjoy. *Lord, Your water is good.*

So how does that illustration of drinking apply to you? You first see Jesus Christ in the Word of God. Then you reach out to Him as one reaches for a cup of water. *Take and receive Him by faith.* As you drink of Jesus, you are receiving Him into your life. "But as many as received Jesus Christ, those people become His children because they believe on Him" (Jn. 1:12, author's translation). So you see, receiving Jesus is believing on Him. And after you take Him into your life, you can enjoy Him.

What should a person drink? As I was speaking to a Southern Baptist ministers' meeting, I mentioned that my pastor drank black coffee when he fasted for 40 days.

"You can't do that!" a voice yelled out from the back of the room. An elderly minister was belligerently trying to tell me my pastor was wrong.

I smiled at what he was trying to say, and then I apologized for not making myself clear so that people could understand me. Then I said again, "My pastor drank nothing but coffee when he fasted 40 days." The crotchety old man yelled out again, "You can't do that!"

I apologized the second time for not making myself clear and repeated the same statement again, "My pastor only drank black coffee when fasting for 40 days." Again the man yelled out, You can't do that!"

Then I corrected the man for his using a wrong word. He had said that my pastor "can't do that" but he should have said, "He shouldn't do that." I reminded the fussy old man that there are three rules you can apply to drinking liquids when fasting.

First is the rule of *non-nutrition*. My pastor says you shouldn't drink anything that is nutritious while fasting, and to him, any type of juice is nutritious. He says that black coffee and Diet Pepsi (colored water) are non-nutritious. So while my pastor fasts, he drinks black coffee and Diet Pepsi.

The second rule is *non-enjoyable*. I don't feel you should drink anything for enjoyment when you are fasting, and diet drinks are in that category for me. When I fasted for 40 days, I drank a glass of orange juice in the morning, and a glass of V-8 juice at night. I didn't deviate to different kinds of juices, which would have been more enjoyable, nor did I try to break a monotonous routine. I drank only what I considered was necessary, but nothing for enjoyment.

The rule of *silence* is the third rule. It's stated, "If God hasn't spoken, don't make rules." The fact is God hasn't made rules concerning what you should drink when you fast. At times of fasting, the Bible says people drank water, at other times it just says they drank. It doesn't

73

say what they drank, so I assume they could have drunk milk, grape juice, or something else. Since God hasn't made a rule about what to drink, we shouldn't make standard rules for everyone to obey

To Take Away

A few will not drink anything when they fast (an absolute fast), which is perfectly acceptable. A few will choose to drink some liquid when fasting. Let God lead you. However, if you're a non-drinker, don't get "super spiritual," thinking the non-drinkers will get closer to God than the drinkers. God doesn't look at what—or how much—goes into the mouth. He looks at what comes out of the heart. The secret of fasting is not withholding food or water; it's hungering and thirsting after righteousness (see Mt. 5:6).

Let's conclude with the subject of drinking by pointing you to everlasting water so you'll never thirst again. That's what Jesus promised (see Jn. 4:14). Fasting does not automatically mean you drink of Him. Fasting will make you thirsty for Him, but you must decide to drink. How do you do that? By immersing yourself in Scripture, by talking to Him, by meditating on Him, and by fellowshipping with Him.

All right, so you've begun a fast. Good! Now you're thirsty for God. Okay. What do you do now? Drink!

NOTES

DRINKING

Chapter 6

DISCIPLINING

I therefore so run, not as uncertainly; so fight I, not as one that beateth the air: but I keep under my body, and bring it into subjection: lest that by any means, when I have preached to others, I myself should be a castaway (1 Corinthians 9:26-27).

Not too far from my home the Virginia Ten Miler is run; this is obviously a ten-mile marathon. Over four thousand runners come from all over the world because it's a registered race, and competing in Lynchburg gives them world rankings, qualifying them for other international races. I admire these runners because they have a discipline *I don't have.*

When I was in high school, I could run ten miles, but now at my age I can barely run the length of a concourse at an airport to catch a plane. I had the ability but lost it. I think I could get it back, but the price is too high. If I gave time and energy to running, I'd take time away from writing, praying, and studying.

Fasting is a discipline, just like running. Fasting is a skill to learn, an art to acquire, and an ability that needs to be trained. Several comparisons can be drawn between acquiring the ability to run and acquiring the ability to fast.

Every fall when I see bronze bodies—perfectly fit—dash past me in their beautiful running outfits, I think, *I can do this. A lot of older men my age do it. Next year I'll do it.* I'm absolutely sincere, and my decision is absolutely captivating. So every year I promise, "Next year I'll run the Ten Miler," but I never do it.

Discipline begins with a decision. Have you made a decision to pursue God? Have you made a decision to fast to know God? Many people have made that decision and they are absolutely sincere, but they never do it. Why? Every race of ten miles begins with a decision to run, and inherent in that decision to run is a second decision to train.

My decision to run the Ten Miler never leads to my running ten miles because I don't follow through with training...practice...routine. Hence, my decision is only a dream. I didn't really decide to run ten miles, I only dreamed about it. Doesn't the Bible say something about "Old men dreaming dreams"?

Even though you've wanted to fast, you've never done so because your decision to fast is only a dream. When you finally begin your first day of fasting, it's like the first day of practice. My first day of running wouldn't be very spectacular because I would only be able to run the length of one block. One block seems like nothing compared to ten miles and so I'd get discouraged with running and quit. Is that why you haven't fasted yet? Fasted more? Fasted until you've gotten through to God? You've quit because you've gotten discouraged. *Lord, give me strength to go on.*

The secret to fasting—like running—is the discipline of daily follow-through. You have to establish a running schedule, a time, a place, and a distance. If you wait to run until you find the extra time, you'll never do it. Same with fasting. You must discipline yourself to fast, and follow-through—a time, a purpose, a plan.

Future dreams are built on daily routines.

As you practice daily, you'll build up your ability to run well and to run farther. You've got to "run through" those bad practice sessions. You've got to do it when you don't feel like it.

You may feel like you accomplish little the first time you fast. But don't obligate yourself to fast just once. Commit yourself to the continual practice of fasting. You'll get better at it and you'll get more out of it. One bad fasting day—headache or internal pain—is no reason to quit the discipline. The next time may be the easiest time ever.

The more you run, the farther you can run. The same with fasting. After you get comfortable with the one-day *Yom Kippur* fast, try a 3-day fast. Then try a 7-day fast...or a 21-day fast...a 40-day fast. However, let me quickly add that the 40-day fast is quite severe. Don't do this unless you're in good physical condition and you have your physician's guidance. Even then, don't attempt it unless you have clear evidence that God is telling you to do so. Most believers don't need to do this. With our busy schedules and complicated lives, most believers would accomplish more with a one-day fast each week for 40 weeks.

You must discipline yourself; God cannot do it for you. If you're training to run the Ten Miler, you have to watch what you eat, and develop a tough mental attitude about your body. You must deny self, practice daily, and get the right amount of sleep. Do you know what this sounds like? It sounds very similar to the instructions that Jesus gave to become one of His disciplined followers:

> *And He said to them all, If any man will come after Me, let him deny himself, and take up his cross daily, and follow Me* (Luke 9:23).

Notice, this Scripture suggests you are responsible to discipline yourself. It's not something you pray, "God do it for me..." It is something you must do for yourself. *You* must deny yourself, *you* must take up your cross of difficulties, *you* must follow, and *you* must practice it daily.

Fasting is a discipline that will help you become a better follower of Jesus.

Certain teachers of the Christian life have emphasized only one side of spirituality. They have taught God's enablement without teaching human response. They have taught that the indwelling Christ will empower us to overcome habits, temptations, and weaknesses. Yes, Christ will give you victory; but that is only half the secret to victory. Two must work together; Christ will do His part, as you do your part. When two people pick up a heavy case, each person should carry half the weight. I have learned over the years that Christ works best in those who yield to Him, trust in Him, follow Him, and discipline themselves for Him. *Lord, I want to partner with You.*

If you're going to run the Ten Miler, you have to get serious about subduing the weaknesses and excuses of the flesh (body). Likewise, those who are going to do something for God, have to get serious about subduing the lust and temptations of the flesh (old nature). Paul also uses the analogy of the physical flesh to picture our problems with our lower nature, also called our old man.

To become disciplined, where can you get the best training? Why don't you begin with Jesus? Why don't you look to His example? *Lord, help me keep up.*

You should not try to discipline yourself ignorantly. You can't beat the flesh into submission. There's a key to properly denying yourself and disciplining your body. First, you need the power of Christ in your heart, so yield to the indwelling Christ. Second, you need to look to Jesus as your example. You should discipline yourself as He did. Let Him teach you obedience for He always obeyed when He lived in the flesh. Let His indwelling presence guide you into a life of discipline: "Though He [Jesus] were a Son, yet learned He obedience by the things which He suffered" (Heb. 5:8). As you learn obedience from Him, you can walk as He walked.

In His earthly life, Jesus was God coming down to earth and living under earthly conditions and earthly circumstances. God expects you to live as Jesus did. He is your example. Young people have asked the question, "What Would Jesus Do?" (WWJD?) That's a good rule for your life. When you face difficult decisions or situations and don't know what to do, find out what Jesus would do. Then do it!

Some people have asked, "WWJD?" and discovered the answer, but didn't have the ability to follow through on His example. For instance, Jesus blessed those who cursed Him. But some Christians don't follow that example. Instead, they get angry at those who curse them. They fight back, and some followers of Jesus even try to get even. Remember, Jesus has called you to follow His example, and you can do it when the power of Jesus in you helps you overcome your weakness. *Lord, help me.*

If you follow the example of Jesus, you cannot act any other way than He would act. Therefore if you are seeking to live as Jesus lived, you must first let Him live in your heart, and secondly, follow His example. When you face failure, allow the indwelling Jesus to live His success through you.

When will He help you? It's not a matter of every once in a while; He can do it day-in day-out, week-in week-out, year-in year-out. When you become discouraged and are ready to give up your attempt to follow Jesus, then you must claim the promise, "I can do all things through Christ which strengtheneth me" (Phil. 4:13).

Remember you cannot live for Christ in your own strength. You must trustfully surrender your life to Him, and let His power flow through you. Then you can do what He would do, act the way He would act, and respond as He would. *Lord, give me strength to live for You.*

Jesus said, "I have given you an example, that ye should do as I have done to you" (Jn. 13:15). The example of Jesus washing His disciples' feet is your challenge to deny yourself and become disciplined. There is very little attractiveness in what Jesus did. He stooped to wash dirty feet, and none of us like to do that. It's so humbling to wait on those who are beneath us. But Jesus did it. He was the Son of God, yet He washed the feet of the twelve disciples, including Judas. What do you think went through the mind of the Lord Jesus as He washed Judas' feet?

Thomas á Kempis suggested none can be a real Christian if they *only* confess their weakness in sin. Kempis who spent his life serving others in the monastery said that we don't attain any *real* conformity to the life of Christ until we also *serve* other people. He pointed out that the Lord said without exception, we should take up our cross, follow Him daily; and if we don't do that, then we are not worthy of Him. Kempis described the life of Christ in us and the life of Christ who was willing to serve through us. If we are not willing to serve other people, then we are not willing to follow His example. Since Jesus washed Judas' feet, what should be our attitude toward our enemies? Kempis continually said the actual imitation of our Lord becomes the banner around which the Church should rally its disciples. *Lord, I want to be like You.*

Discipline requires self-denial. Note what Paul said to us about self-denial: "We then that are strong ought to bear the infirmities of the weak, and not to please ourselves. Let every one of us please his neighbor...For even Christ pleased not Himself" (Rom. 15:1-3a). If the life of Jesus Christ is our rule and example, how can we say that we are Christians when we please ourselves first, others second, and Christ seldom? *Lord, forgive me when I put self first.*

The Christian who models Christ as his pattern cannot be content to go through life merely eating, drinking, and having fun. Because Christ did not think of Himself when He suffered for our salvation, neither should we put self first. Just as Christ surrendered Himself to pay for our salvation, so we must surrender ourselves to follow Him explicitly.

When we discipline ourselves in following Christ, we deny our lustful temptations. We do not pay attention to the voice of physical appetites. This is called crucifying our lust. This is what Paul meant when he said, "God forbid that I should glory, save in the cross of our Lord Jesus Christ, by whom the world is crucified unto me, and I unto the world" (Gal. 6:14). When you refuse to feed your lust, you "crucify" your lust. *Lord, I die in Your presence.*

You must deny your lusts and the temptations that come from your old nature, and nail them to the cross. Isn't that what you do when you fast? Once your old nature has been nailed to the cross, you must not take it down to fondle it or serve it.

Paul reminds us, "I am crucified with Christ: nevertheless I live; yet not I, but Christ liveth in me: and the life which I now live in the flesh I live by the faith of the Son of God, who loved me, and gave Himself for me" (Gal. 2:20). You can learn three things from this verse. First, you have been co-crucified with Jesus Christ on the cross. All the benefits of His death are yours. That is a completed action. Second, just as Christ received resurrection life as He came out of the grave, so you receive that same power to live for God and overcome the temptations that face you. Third, you can live by the faith of Jesus Christ. Do you?

When you take up your cross, deny yourself, and follow Him daily; you are following the rule of self-sacrifice that drove Jesus Christ to the cross. Will you live by the rule of self-sacrifice? What have you sacrificed lately? Will you do it by fasting?

Self-denial doesn't always have to do with what is sinful or unlawful; sometimes it means giving up perfectly good things just to seek His presence. There's nothing wrong with eating food; God has provided food for us to eat. But you can follow the law of self-denial when you give up good food to seek His presence. This leads to a disciplined life. *Lord, I will give up good things for You.*

When you fast, you follow the holy rule of Him who said, "Man shall not live by bread alone, but by every word that proceedeth out of the mouth of God" (Mt. 4:4b). What are you doing to feed on His Word so that you may live closer to Him?

Self-denial is also more than denying your fleshly appetites exclusively. Self-denial involves the mind, emotions, and the spirit. You give up your own thoughts to think His thoughts. You give up your own reputation to live for Him. Why? "We...ought...not to please ourselves.... For even Christ pleased not Himself" (Rom. 15:1,3a). Just as self-denial was the law of His life, will you make it the law of your life?

You should find ways to practice self-denial. When you take control of your outer body, you find power to take control of your inner man. And when you can control your physical body, you have taken a valuable step to spirituality. When you have practiced self-denial, you count nothing as a sacrifice for Jesus' sake, and you are never surprised by what other people do. You can expect any and everything from other people. Why? Because you take your orders from Jesus Christ as you walk with Him and obey Him. Nothing else matters.

When you take control
of your physical body, you gain strength
to take control of your mind and emotions.

Fasting is holy poverty. You don't fast to make your-self weak, but to build your character. Fasting is holy hunger, not to make you famished, but to make you holy. Fasting may include a little suffering, but more impor-tantly you are following the example of His holy suffering who bore all our sins in His own body on the tree. Even as He patiently endured affliction for us, so in one sense fasting is patiently enduring afflictions. Why? Paul said, "That I may know Him, and the power of His resurrec-tion, and the fellowship of His sufferings, being made conformable unto His death" (Phil. 3:10). *Lord, I will be hungry to know You better.*

What happens when you take up your cross and fol-low Jesus? With the power of self-denial, you have the ability to reach into Heaven through Jesus Christ and touch the heart of God. When is the last time you touched God? When is the last time you could say, *"Jesus only* in my life"? *Lord, I say it now.*

Self-denial is not merely a negative victory over sin, the flesh, and the devil. You are not solely trying to defeat them, nor is your only goal to keep your life clean. Your primary goal is to have Jesus Christ sitting on the throne at the center of your heart. So ask yourself, "Who sits on the throne of my heart?" When He has His right place in the center of your life, nothing else matters. Lord, sit on the throne of my life.

To Take Away

What does it take to become a great pianist? Well, you must have tremendous raw talent. But that won't achieve greatness without hours of toiling practice. It is the same when wanting to become like Jesus. You are given His nature in your new birth, but to live like Jesus, you must practice discipline and self-denial...hours of toiling practice. You must take up your cross, deny yourself, follow Jesus, and practice it daily.

On the other hand, some have raw ability and they also practice a lot, yet they still never become great pianists. Why? No desire! No passion! They don't want it badly enough. Again, the same pattern holds true in the Christian life. To live like Jesus, you must want to be like Jesus. And the more you want to be like Jesus, the more you can become like Him. Who do you want to be like? How much will you deny yourself to become like Him?

NOTES

DISCIPLINING

Chapter 7

GROWING

Behold, there went out a sower to sow: and it came to pass, as he sowed, some fell by the way side, and the fowls of the air came and devoured it up. And some fell on stony ground, where it had not much earth; and immediately it sprang up, because it had no depth of earth: but when the sun was up, it was scorched; and because it had no root, it withered away. And some fell among thorns, and the thorns grew up, and choked it, and it yielded no fruit. And other fell on good ground, and did yield fruit that sprang up and increased; and brought forth, some thirty, and some sixty, and some an hundred (Mark 4:3-8).

S ome people are like azalea bushes planted on the sand of an ocean beach where they will never flourish because that soil has no life-giving nutrition. Nothing grows on a sandy beach but a few scrubby weeds. Likewise, an azalea bush planted among rocks will die because the shallow depth of soil provides no nourishment for the bush's roots. And unfortunately, an azalea bush settled among briars and weeds will be choked to death. Some people will never mature in Christ because they neglect to plant themselves in a place where they can grow.

Planting yourself in the soils of life. If you plant your life in the sand of fun and relaxation, you deny yourself the nutrition of the Word of God, prayer, and fellowship with Jesus Christ. Subsequently, you will never grow, but will eventually die. If you plant your life in the middle of a packed rocky roadway of business and activities, there will be no way for your roots to reach deep into life-giving soil so you can survive the blistering sun of persecution, or those long dry spells when reinvigorating rain doesn't reach you. And then again, if you are planted among sinful thorns and briars, any potential growth will be surely choked away. But if you send your roots deep into the nutritious soil of God Himself, it is then that you will be nourished and grow.

Leave the growing to God. Have you ever seen a lily trying to make itself grow? You can preach to lilies, "Try real hard to grow!" but your preaching won't help. And even if lilies could command themselves to grow, your preaching still wouldn't help. Jesus said that the lilies do not spin or toil (see Mt. 6:28). He meant that lilies do not try to grow; they just grow. And what did He mean when He said, "Even Solomon in all his glory was not [as beautiful as these lilies]" (Lk. 12:27 NKJV)? He meant only God can make a beautiful flower. Would you like to grow? Would you like to be a beautiful flower for God? Then, what must you do? Plant yourself in His presence, and then leave "the growing" to God. *Lord, I want to grow.*

While lilies grow to become beautiful flowers, they're not concerned about becoming what they're not, nor are they concerned about how quickly they're growing. They just do their "lily thing." The Lord said that if you will "abide in Me and I in you" (Jn. 15:4a), then you can grow. It seems to me when you abide in Christ, you're like a lily abiding in the growth pattern that is given by God. You'll simply grow. *Lord, I'll abide.*

Growing spiritually is not self-effort to become a better man of God or a woman of prayer; but rather growing is yielding to the inward life principle that God has put within your heart. You must know who you are in God's order. How do you find out? You learn by fasting, talking to God, listening to God, re-directing your life, and resting in His blueprint for your life.

Transforming your poor dirt into rich soil. Perhaps you are not growing in grace because you are planted in poor soil. Maybe you've been planted under some bushes where the sun doesn't reach you to bring out all the colors of your potential. Do you feel like you've been planted in a beach or among bricks on a sidewalk? Maybe you think it's impossible to transform poor dirt into good soil. Listen to this story.

My mother grew up on a farm in South Carolina, but moved to the city-living of Savannah, Georgia, when she married. She didn't forget her heritage though, and always grew a vegetable garden in the backyard. Her green thumb was her signature in life. After a series of rental homes, she finally bought a house and a two-acre plot of ground on the edge of town; but the backyard was as sandy as the ocean beach 20 miles away. Nothing of value would grow, only weeds. But she wouldn't let any obstacle keep her from growing her vegetables.

She contacted a handyman who worked yards and cut grass. At her request, he dumped all his leaves and grass cuttings in my mother's backyard. The handyman had a mule that he used to plow the leaves under the soil where they would rot to form compost. At times the backyard was covered with two feet of leaves and grass. Eventually, as the leaves rotted, our sandy backyard became rich black soil. The ground became the richest in the neighborhood, and our neighbors remarked of my mother, "She could grow tomatoes on a hoe handle stuck in the ground."

What about you? Does the soil around you need to be transformed? You can't do it, but I know a Divine Gardener who can. He can transform any life by first transforming your heart, and second, by transforming your surroundings. *Lord, transform the soil of my heart.*

That doesn't mean the Gardener will make you financially rich so that you can purchase the best farm in the state. But when you take time to fast and seek His presence, you will grow to become godly: "You become like the Lord by beholding His glory in a mirror" (2 Cor 3:18, author's translation).

Growing God's Way. Lilies don't grow like pine trees, and no matter how hard they try, they can never grow to become a pine tree. A beautiful lily comes from the seed of a lily and will always be a lily. If you want to grow spiritually, you must grow God's way established for you. It is His life that causes you to grow to be like Him and to grow according to the seed that is planted in your heart. When you experience His love, it brings out love in you. *Lord, make me like You.*

Have you ever noticed how a lily graces the smallest corner given to it? It doesn't try to be an orchid on a vine, nor does it try to be a beautiful magnolia growing high in the trees. A lily is most attractive when it is naturally beautiful. Why can't you be that way?

You must put aside your own growth agenda, and grow God's way. Jesus said, "Think about how the lilies grow" (Lk. 12:27, author's translation). God gives His total attention to growing the tiniest lily. The Mighty God of Heaven, who created this large planet in the universe, will also give all His attention to make you the most beautiful flower in the world.

Still growing when it storms. A lily doesn't worry about blowing winds or falling rain. As a matter of fact, it seems that no matter how hard the winds blow, or how much rain falls upon it, a lily still blooms with all its beauty. Can you do that with your job pressures blowing upon you?

What happens when the storms of temptation pour buckets of rain upon you? *Lord, protect me from the storm.*

Dead plants can't grow. Suppose you try to make a dead flower grow. You water it, fertilize it, and even allow the warm life-giving sun of God to shine upon it. Even with all this care and nourishment, a dead flower still can't grow.

Maybe you're not growing in Christ because you're dead at the center. Outwardly, you appear religious; everyone knows that you have joined the church, and that you can sing the praises of God. But when the water of God's Word is poured upon you and the sun of prayer shines upon you, nothing happens because inwardly you're dead.

You need to be "born again" into God's family to grow. First you are born physically into your parent's family, and then you can be "born again" into God's family. "But as many as received Him, to them He gave the right to become children of God, to those who believe in His name" (Jn. 1:12 NKJV).

If you want to grow, you must first become God's child. You do that by receiving Jesus Christ into your heart. When you're born again, you receive God's life; you receive eternal life. Whether you consciously try or not, you cannot make a dead tree grow, just like you cannot make a person without the life of God live for Him. But a live flower just naturally grows because of what's on the inside. Do you naturally grow?

To Take Away

Would you be satisfied if your little child remained a cute cuddly baby all of his life, and never grew? What farmer would be satisfied if his grain were planted, but never grew, reached full height and never produced fruit?

"But grow in grace, and in the knowledge of our Lord and Savior Jesus Christ" (2 Pet. 3:18a). This command applies to all of us. There is a life of faith that is available to every believer, and God has made it possible that you can follow to know God and grow in Him.

NOTES

GROWING

Chapter 8

LOOKING

Wherefore seeing we also are compassed about with so great a cloud of witnesses, let us lay aside every weight, and the sin which doth so easily beset us, and let us run with patience the race that is set before us, looking unto Jesus the author and finisher of our faith; who for the joy that was set before Him endured the cross, despising the shame, and is set down at the right hand of the throne of God (Hebrews 12:1-2).

F asting is looking beyond the things you can see in this world and looking to the unseen spiritual world; it is looking to Jesus. But when you look to Jesus, why are you looking? Where are you looking? What do you see?

Looking for protection. As a young kid, I was a member of a mischievous group of boys who called ourselves The Cat Patrol. We never got into much trouble. Actually, the worst thing we ever did was sandbag the house of a cranky old man on Halloween. Like any group of mischievous boys, we didn't want any parents snooping around our treehouse, so we always posted a *lookout*. When I was the lookout, I watched for any adults or girls—one was as snoopy as the other.

Why did we post a lookout? To protect ourselves. What were we looking out for? Perceived danger. What did we see? Nothing. While we were not really in any danger, we continually played this game and life was fun.

Maybe you want to protect yourself from something you fear, and so you fast. The word *fasting* comes from the Hebrew *tsum*, which means "distress" or "loss of appetite during time of danger or threat." If you heard your spouse was in an accident and was in the emergency room at the hospital, what would you do? You'd rush to the hospital. But if it were noon, would you drive through to get a hamburger on the way to the hospital? No! Thinking only of the emergency, you'd forget your hunger. When something scares you, you lose your appetite. Maybe you're scared of a cancer intruding your body...Fast! Maybe you're afraid of losing your job...Fast! Fast and look to God to intervene. When you are frightened, remember why you fast. You're looking to God.

Looking for deliverance. At one time in the Scriptures a *look* was necessary to save a person from death. Because Israel had sinned against God, "fiery serpents" came into the camp, and their stinging bite proved deadly. However, Israel repented, "We have sinned" (see Num. 21:7). And so God told Moses to make a brass serpent—a symbol of their sin: "Make a fiery serpent, and set it on a pole; and it shall be that everyone who is bitten, when he looks at it, shall live" (Num. 21:8 NKJV). All they had to do was look and live. Jesus used this story to explain that *looking was believing* (see Jn. 3:14-16). When you get in trouble, look to Jesus.

Perhaps you're afraid of God because of what you've done. You've disobeyed Him. "Moses...was afraid to look upon God" (Ex. 3:6b). Do you realize that when you refuse to look to God, it's disobedience? God says, "Look unto Me, and be ye saved...for I am God" (Is. 45:22a). *Lord, I look to You for forgiveness.*

Looking is anticipation. As a Boeing 747 descends from the sky, a notice flashes on the airport lobby sign, "Flight 351...Just Arrived." You stand and begin to pace, anticipating the sight of a loved one you haven't seen for a long time. You've hoped for this day to come, and now you're overwhelmed with the thought that in just a few moments, your longing will be fulfilled.

In the same way, as you fast, you greatly long for the presence of God. You are filled with joy and excitement and look forward to being with Him. You anticipate His goodness and desire His company.

Unfortunately there are some who never bother to look to God for their daily life. They live as though there is no God. What will happen to those who aren't looking? They will be caught as a thief, who has no lookout, who is seized and arrested by the police. If you're not looking for the return of Jesus, you will be surprised when He appears.

"The Lord...will come in a day when you don't look for Him" (Mt. 24:50, author's translation).

Only a few are looking. What is God to most people, including many Christians? Some say that because this is such a big powerful world that couldn't have possibly created itself, there must have been a big powerful God who is its Creator. So they reason and decide, "We must believe there is a God." They make Him a conclusion. But they only know about the God of creation; they don't really *know* Him.

I say there is a God because I know Him.

To others in the church, God is just an idea. Anything in their mind is a thought. They rationalize that if they can think about God, He is an idea. Again, they know about God rationally, but they don't *know* Him. But, I know Him because I talk to God.

A few go even further. They declare that they believe in God by their creeds. They confess, "I believe in God the Father Almighty, Maker of Heaven and earth." Their speech declares that they know God, but in their experience, God is no more real to them than any other thing in the unseen world. They go through life trying to love the idea of God, or they try to believe in the principle of God.

I love God because I have experienced God.

Is God a person we can look for? Is God a person who can be known...can be experienced...can be seen? He did walk in the Garden of Eden to talk with Adam. If God is a person who we can know, then He has a mind, which is the first quality of personhood. He has rationality and we can talk to Him as He talks to us. When's the last time you talked to God? *Hello, God, I need to talk with You.*

The second quality of personhood is emotions or feelings. God loves, for I have felt His loving kindness. He also hates. He detests sin, and I have felt His severe rebuke when I've tolerated sin in my life. Therefore, I've learned to come to God as a sensitive person...to feel His presence...to experience His passion...to enjoy His person. *Lord, I want to feel You.*

The third quality of personhood is volition or will. God is not bound, but He is free to make choices. He has volition. Sometimes I try to get Him to bend His will to answer my prayers. But I find I must learn to bend my will to His. Evan Roberts, the preacher who initiated the great Wales Revival of 1904, prayed, "Bend me, Lord; bend me." *Lord, that's my prayer.*

You can know God to the same degree of intimacy that you know other people. And who do you know best of all in life? Is it your mother? Your spouse? Or one of your children? You can have the same intimate relationship with God that you have with another person. *Oh God, I want to know You.*

Looking includes our five senses. Because God is a person, we can relate to Him as we relate to the world through our five senses—sight, sound, taste, touch, and smell. How do we relate to God through these five senses? Notice Jesus includes *sound*, "My sheep hear My voice" (Jn. 10:27a). He also mentions *sight*, "Blessed are the pure in heart: for they shall see God" (Mt. 5:8). We can figuratively *taste* God, "Taste and see that the Lord is good" (Ps. 34:8a) and *smell* Him, "All Thy garments smell of myrrh, and aloes, and cassia, out of the ivory palaces" (Ps. 45:8a). And can we touch Him with our hands? No. But we can touch His heart with our hearts. *Thank You, God, for touching me in all my senses.*

The sixth sense. At the heart of the Christian faith is our belief that we can look into the invisible world. We believe that there is a God we can't see with physical eyes. Yet through a sixth sense, we can see God. Just as we understand the physical world by our senses, so can we experience and know God through our sixth sense. Paul claims that the "eyes of your understanding [may be] enlightened" (Eph. 1:18a).

At the same time, God continues to speak to us through our five senses, the windows to our soul. We believe that God sees everything we do, hears us when we pray, and guides our every step. So if we believe there is an invisible world, why do we act as though the world that we can touch is the only world there is? Maybe it's because the physical world—the one we can see, touch, hear, smell, and experience—demands our attention.

Many people deny the existence of God because they can't interact with Him using their five senses. They say there is no God because they can't see Him, touch Him, smell Him, taste Him, or hear Him. But these are not the only ways we can communicate with God. Through the sixth sense, we can know God in our heart. *God, I know You exist because You hear me when I talk to You.*

Looking to the spiritual kingdom. There is a spiritual kingdom where God is about us, over us, under us, and before us, guiding our life. God Himself is waiting for you to look to Him. Why don't you begin searching for Him now?

In our limited thinking, we tend to draw a false contrast between God's spiritual world and God's natural world about us. Because we can't see God, we think these two worlds can't co-exist. The imaginary line we've drawn to separate this world from the spiritual world is just that—imaginary...not real.

Ah, but when you begin to think that there is a line, at least you are admitting there is another life; there is a kingdom of God out there. So, if He's out there, do you want to know Him? Maybe you need God and you need Him now. You're in a mess and you want God to come help get rid of your troubles. If you're in danger, you don't just want a knowledge of God or a feeling about God in another world. You need Him now...in this world. You want Him to leave the other world to come to you in this world. If you look for Him, you can find Him. *Lord, there You are!*

The trouble is we have a bad habit of ignoring the spiritual world about us, and we don't pay any attention to God who is in *that* world or *this* world. So, begin looking to God by fasting. He will come to you and He will help you. Remember what the Bible promises, "He that cometh to God must believe that He is, and that He is a rewarder of them that diligently seek Him" (Heb. 11:6b).

Jesus said to begin by acknowledging He exists. He said, "You believe in God" (Jn. 14:1b). Then He gave a command, "Believe also in Me" (Jn. 14:1b). Without acknowledging the first, you can't enter into the life of the second. You must believe or acknowledge God, then you come to Him through Jesus. "Jesus saith...I am the way, the truth, and the life: no man cometh unto the Father, but by Me" (Jn. 14:6). Then only through the second—Jesus Christ—do you fully acknowledge the first—God.

You must choose which one of the two worlds will direct your life. If you choose Christ, you deliberately choose the spiritual kingdom of God. If you choose the physical world, you are deliberately denying the spiritual world, the other world of God. If you want to know God, you must choose the world unseen with physical eyes; you must seek Him with your spiritual eyes.

Some Christians mistakenly believe that the spiritual world is *out there,* and so it will come sometime in the future. They dream of Heaven after they die where they will live with God forever. As a result, these people have very little relationship with God in this present world. They're waiting for the sound of the trumpet, and a voice to call them up higher. But is that enough? What about today? Can the kingdom of God be here and now? *Lord, I want to see You now.*

To Take Away

Your soul has eyes to see God, and ears to hear God. "But blessed are your eyes, for they see: and your ears, for they hear" (Mt. 13:16).

When you begin to focus upon God, you begin to see His will for your life; you begin to hear His inner voice guiding you, and more than that; you begin to touch God and be touched by Him. As you eat His food, and smell His fragrance, you know God intimately. When that happens, and a *God-consciousness* captures your awareness; then inwardly, you will feel God for who He is and see God for what He can do for you.

NOTES

LOOKING

Chapter 9

RESTING

Come unto Me, all ye that labour and are heavy laden, and I will give you rest. Take My yoke upon you, and learn of Me; for I am meek and lowly in heart: and ye shall find rest unto your souls (Matthew 11:28-29).

When I was a teenager I rode my bicycle all the way across Georgia and South Carolina in the summertime. During those hot blistering days, I would come upon an old-fashioned country gas station with a shaded driveway. After a few minutes of rest in the shade and a cool drink, I was renewed for my next 20 miles of hot highway. In the same way, as you walk through the trials of this life, a little rest can renew your spirit for the next challenge, and a little shade can keep you going.

Listen to the promise of Jesus, "...My grace is sufficient for thee: for My strength is made perfect in weakness.

[Paul responds] Most gladly therefore will I rather glory in my infirmities, that the power of Christ may rest upon me" (2 Cor. 12:9). Because Jesus is gracious, He allows His power to rest on us. The word *rest* (*epi*, upon; *skene*, a tent) has the unique meaning of "spreading a tent over me." What does Jesus do when you are tired, worn out, and can't take another step? He spreads a tent so you can rest. Fasting provides that cool resting place on a hot journey. When you fast, "the power of Christ rests upon you."

Next time you come apart from the heavy pressures of this world, rest in the Lord Jesus Christ. Stop pushing ahead, and rest alongside the road. Begin to fast and the Lord will cover you with His tabernacle of shade so you can be refreshed to return to the grind of work. *Lord, there's a little shade up the road; can I stop awhile and rest?*

What is rest? Rest is a quality of life that unsaved people do not know about, and most Christians have not experienced. After God completed the work of Creation in six days, He rested. "Thus the heavens and the earth, and all the host of them, were finished. And on the seventh day God ended His work which He had done, and He rested on the seventh day from all His work which He had done" (Gen. 2: 1-2 NKJV). Why did God rest? Obviously, God didn't rest because He was exhausted; although sometimes *you* need rest when you're tired. And obviously, God didn't rest because He needed to renew His spent energy; whereas sometimes *you* need rest to replenish your strength. And there are other times *you* rest because you're sick and need to break a fever or overcome a disease. Obviously, this also was not God's purpose for resting. Still further, sometimes *you* rest to prepare yourself for hard work. This reason, of course, could not have been why God rested *after* Creation.

God's rest is peace, calmness, and serenity where you are in control of yourself and situation. Nothing is out of place, everything is right, and you are not threatened or pressured to do anything.

God rested because rest is what God does and who God is. When God rests, He is completely in control of Himself, and He controls all the world about Him. Everything is right, and He doesn't need to do anything else. *Lord, I want to rest, just like You rested.*

Two kinds of rest. There is a rest that you will experience after completing your life on earth. All believers who die will enter that rest—the rest of Heaven. Our other rest is an analogy; it is the rest we have on earth. This rest is not a complete rest, nor is it a final rest. But it is a wonderful rest. When you experience tensions on this earth, you can enter into *His rest.* This is the rest promised by Jesus Christ. You receive rest through the Word of God, as you fast and read the Bible. You get rest through prayer as you fast and talk to Jesus. You obtain rest through surrender as you fast and yield your life up to Him. *Lord, I surrender all.*

Spiritual rest. You encounter spiritual rest in the Lord when you fast. And why is that? Fasting is a life-giving experience. When you fast, you give life to your soul and spirit; you renew yourself. While you can fast for physical reasons, such as breaking an addiction, meeting a financial need, or receiving an answer to an impossible prayer, there is a fast to know God intimately. It is this fast that leads to rest.

Many people don't consider that you could ever gain rest from fasting; they instead dwell on the supposition that strength is being sapped from their body and pleasure is being denied from their taste buds because they are not eating. Rather, the opposite takes place. You enter into the rest that the Lord gives you. When Jesus said, "Take My rest upon you," He did not intend that you should take a rest from work or a rest from your daily activities. But rather, you should rest from struggling with sin, rest from your wild imaginations, rest from your condemning conscience, and give rest to your striving heart. Finding rest in Jesus Christ is the ideal place for soul satisfaction. *Lord, I feel good in Your presence.*

What does it mean when the Scripture promises, "There remaineth therefore a rest to the people of God" (Heb. 4:9)? The word "rest" here is *sabbatismos* which is a "Sabbath rest." This means much more than keeping the Sabbath laws. When God promises rest to His people, He declares they will (a) cease their work, (b) fellowship with the Lord, and (c) do what He did after creating the world. The *rest* is the rest of God Himself. *Rest* is what He did, and *rest* is what He offers you. When you rest in the Lord, you possess His life in you, and His work flows through you. When you enter into divine rest, you enter into God Himself, and you do what God did. *Lord, I'm coming to rest in You.*

Fasting is so much more than not eating. By yielding to God and letting Him flow through you, you can enjoy rest and experience a oneness with God not previously felt.

Don't measure your fasting
by the food you give up, but
by the fellowship you gain with God.

When are you going to rest? Some people, like Solomon, can be characterized as "a man of rest" (see 1 Chron. 22:9). Solomon's father, David, had been a man of war. He had killed many and conquered much. But once Israel's enemies were defeated and David passed from the scene, then came the calm kingdom of Solomon. He was a man of peace and rest, with no battles to fight. Are you characterized as a person of peace and rest like Solomon? Or are you considered to be a person of battles and wars? Do you continually strive for more material possessions...a bigger car, a bigger house? Do you constantly strive after promotions? Will you always want better...but you're not sure what better means? You can become a person of rest as you fast. Why? Because you put aside the most basic human pursuit of all—food; and you pursue God for who He is. *Lord, make me a person of rest.*

Resting for refreshment. When we rest, we are refreshed. Paul says in Second Corinthians 7:13b, "Because his [Titus] spirit was refreshed by you all." Titus received something from the believers at Corinth—he was refreshed. What can that mean to you? When you seek God and fast with Him, you can be refreshed. If you are tired, your vigor will be restored. Have you felt a little dull and discouraged in your Christian walk? Then fast to be revived.

Not only will your spirit be restored, but your body also will be refreshed when you fast. Your digestive system rests, as well as the pressures of your heart, lungs, and elimination system. Without having to struggle to ingest new food, the whole body takes a rest.

The word *refreshed* also means to grasp a new vision of what you can accomplish. Tired aching bones and muscles remind you of things you can't do. But rest and refreshment will enable you to assume responsibility for bigger tasks with the assurance you can do it. So fast if you have soul-aches, and fast if you are ministry-tired. Do you need refreshment? Fast to restore strength in God Himself.

Resting from your struggle. Some of you are still struggling with the battles of life. Perhaps you are fighting addiction, or maybe you're struggling because someone has lied about you. Maybe someone wants your job. So you're striving just to hang on. Rest is available to you. Jesus said, "Come unto Me, all ye that labour and are heavy laden, and I will give you rest" (Mt. 11:28). Jesus is speaking to those whose lives are filled with anxiety. Although the things people struggled with in Jesus' day might have been different than our day, the internal pressure is fundamentally the same. Whether is it the "lust of the eyes, the lust of the flesh, or the pride of life," we all struggle to overcome our weakness and sinful nature. If you're still struggling with your desires, consider God's promise: "Therefore, since a promise remains of entering His rest, let us fear lest any of you seem to have come short of it" (Heb. 4:1 NKJV). God assures that He will give you rest.

Where is rest found? In Jesus! Remember His invitation, "Come unto Me." How do you get close to Jesus? When you fast to seek His presence, you move beyond singing about Him in church and hearing about Him in a sermon. In the privacy of your quiet time, you intimately talk with Him. When you fast, you stop pleasing the body and you seek to please God Himself. When was the last time you had an intimate talk with Jesus?

Resting to overcome work, pain, or battle. Have you ever worked in the yard until you were so tired you had difficulty standing up? Even after you were exhausted, you drove yourself to cut just a little more of the lawn to finish the job. Maybe you were digging a hole and had just a few more feet to shovel. Maybe you were driving home late at night and didn't want to stop and check into a motel. Whatever the occasion, you pushed your body past the limits. Even though you couldn't take it any longer, you still pressed a little farther. In that excruciating experience, what you wanted most of all was rest.

Let's relate this physical pain to spiritual pain. Have you ever struggled against a problem that you didn't know what to do? Have you ever fought against a habit so much that you wanted to die? What must you do? Fast. When you fast, you turn your back on the pressures of this world. You completely yield yourself and your future to God, then you determine to follow God's principles to trust Him with your future. You find rest when you enter this commitment experience. You enter the same kind of experience when you commit yourself to fast for deliverance from spiritual pressures. God promises, "There remaineth therefore a rest to the people of God" (Heb. 4:9). *Lord, I'm tired.*

Earlier we described rest as a quality of God. This means that when you fast, you enter into God's rest and begin to experience your world the way God sees things and feel about your world. Your victory is not in your rest, but *your victory is in His rest.*

When rest is necessary. There are times when rest is not just something to be enjoyed or desired, it is absolutely necessary. When Jesus saw the weariness of His disciples in ministry, He said, "...Come...apart...and rest a while" (Mk. 6:31a). He knew they needed rest and He went with them because He also needed rest. Rest was getting away from the ministry that was draining them of their strength and determination. *Lord, I'm drained.*

Fasting can allow you to get away from your humdrum existence, or remove yourself from the pressures of life. When you fast from earthly food, you feed upon the

Bread of Life, the Lord Jesus Christ, and you drink the water of life, the Holy Spirit. When you just can't go any farther, you need to "come apart" and fast awhile. There you'll find rest.

Rest prepares you for the future. To make it through some days, you need a little rest in the middle of the afternoon. Those few moments of rest give you strength to complete the day. Most Americans call it "coffee break." Whether you're sweating out in the sun, or sitting in an air-conditioned office, you need a rest break to revive your spirit and direct your focus to the next task. Perhaps that's what fasting will do for you. When you need to get ready for the next great task, fast for it.

An example of fasting to prepare for the future is illustrated many years ago when I wrote the program *Friend Day*, which was sold to over 40,000 churches. It was a plan of friendship evangelism that involved every person in a church bringing a friend on a special day called Friend Day. The purpose was to win people to Christ through existing relationships. I instructed the pastors to take off either Friday or Saturday before *Friend Day* to spend the day in fasting and prayer for a successful campaign. Because there would be many unsaved people in church, the pastor needed the power of God on his ministry. Is that power also available to you? Yes, by prayer and fasting. You can prepare for your next level of service by fasting and prayer. *Lord, I will prepare for the giant challenges of life by fasting.*

Resting makes you feel good. How do you feel when you work all day? Whether you've had pressure at the office or your muscles ache from physical work, you usually look forward to going to bed and resting. Usually when I am tired the most, I enjoy my bed the most. For the first few moments after I crawl between clean sheets, I relish the experience. I can feel every muscle in my body relaxing; it's as though I am slowly sinking into the mattress. In just a short time, the inviting sheets are warmed by my body temperature. Then in that toasty cocoon, I enjoy my comfy bed. It doesn't take long before I drift into sleep and I get rest for the next day.

In the same way, I look forward to fasting and communion with God. There are some people that feel that fasting is physical pain, or even torture. I find it a comfortable experience.

Sometimes I have to admit that my calendar squeezes my quiet time. I wake up in the morning and immediately think about an important meeting I need to attend or a lecture I want to review. So, I consider hurrying through my quiet time with God so that I can get on with my life. It's then that I have to learn the lesson of seeking God for the pleasure of His company. It's then I gain the rest from Him that makes me feel good for the day. *Lord, I feel comfortable in Your presence.*

Resting is a command. Fasting is not an easy thing to do because your physical body cries out, "I'm hungry." But you obey the command of God, "Seek ye My face," and you respond like the Psalmist, "Thy face, Lord, will I seek" (Ps. 27:8). Even though *you* have chosen to stop eating to seek God, it is God who motivates you to go without food to seek His face. You must understand, "It is God which worketh in you both to will and to do of His *good pleasure*" (Phil. 2:13, emphasis mine). We are commanded to, "Rest in the Lord, and wait patiently for Him" (Ps. 37:7a). Since we are commanded to rest in the Lord, we know that rest is obtainable. Are you tired today? Why don't you rest in God. *Lord, I'm tired, refresh me.*

Restoring your soul. When you are spiritually drained, what do you do? Fast! When you feel your heart is empty so that your prayers bounce off the ceiling, what do you do? Fast! When you learn that the Lord is your Shepherd, then you find yourself saying, "I shall not want." When you find yourself following your Shepherd beside still waters, what do you receive? "He restoreth my soul" (see Ps. 23).

Notice what the Shepherd will do to draw you close to Him. The Bible says, "He maketh me to lie down." He "makes" you lie down in green pastures where there is food for you to eat—He makes you rest. The Shepherd does not pull your legs out from under you so that you drop down, nor does He push you over until you fall down. How then does He do it? He leads me to green pastures where there is food. Since I am hot and tired, I will naturally want to lie down in the cool green grass to get something to eat. Because I'm tired, I want to lie down. He doesn't force me to lie down; He leads me to green pastures where He knows I'll naturally lie down.

God does not force you to fast, but He will make you tired so that you will want to rest in Him. It is then you fast. He makes you hungry, then leads you to the place where you want to eat. Have you been eating spiritual food lately? Have you been enjoying His presence? If not, follow Him beside still waters so you can have rest. *Lord, make a place for me to lie down, I'm coming to You.*

Notice Psalm 23 doesn't describe the Lord leading you by the oceans to tempt you to go swimming nor does He lead you by a powerful rushing river to teach you about His magnificent creative ability. He doesn't even lead you by a waterfall so you can enjoy its artistic beauty. He leads you by still waters so you can rest. Maybe even sleep. *It's restful here in Your presence, Lord; why can't I stay here?*

A shepherd doesn't let his sheep stay by still waters though. He leads you *beside* the still waters, which means He leads you past still waters, back out into the hectic world. You can't fast forever, and you can't spend all day in your quiet time. He will lead you to the still waters, then lead you away from still waters. You go there to rest and drink, and then you need to move on with your life. *Lord, it's hard to leave Your presence.*

You can't live forever in a monastery, you've got a job and work to do. You may have a family that needs your care. So the Lord leads you beside still waters, which means you can rest a day or two, or a week or two, to be restored to move on. "But Lord, it's so good to stay here, why can't we pitch a tent here like Peter wanted to pitch a tent on the Mount of Transfiguration?" (Mt. 17:4, author's translation).

You come into His presence to get rest and revitalization, then it's time to move on. You fast to learn how the Lord leads and where the Lord leads, then pack up your tent to go about your obligations.

Rest from the tyranny of sin and slavery. Sin is not a kind master. First it flirts with you by enticement, and then attracts you with its pleasures. But like a hot bath, it's not so hot after you're in for awhile. Sin is not alluring once you drink deeply. In fact, sin is a very hard taskmaster that will physically brutalize you, emotionally devastate you, and spiritually bankrupt you.

For those in sin God says, "...Stand ye in the ways, and see, and ask for the old paths, where is the good way, and walk therein, and ye shall find rest for your souls..." (Jer. 6:16). This rest is not for those on the journey of faith, but for those who are wrestling with sin. This is the rest *from* sin, this is the rest that you get from repentance.

Perhaps you are addicted and can't break from those chains. You used to be free, but now you are enslaved to your habit. You used to take a drink of liquor, but now drink takes you. You sucked on a cigarette, but now you are the addicted sucker. Your integrity has been drugged, and you have been dragged through the streets. What do you do?

You fast to break addiction, however this is not an easy fast, nor is it an automatic success. Just as addiction came one cigarette at a time, so freedom comes one step at a time. That means that spiritual freedom comes one day at a time. Even when you get victory, it is temporary; you enjoy victory one day at a time.

I think it might be better for the person who has been addicted physically to drugs, alcohol, or tobacco, to fast one day each week for 40 weeks, rather than fast once for 40 days. However, all addictions are different, and you may need to fast differently. I don't recommend any fasting for 40 days without seriously considering what you are doing and being carefully led of the Lord. Only a few should attempt this fast because it is so severe. But on the other hand, it may take that severe prescription to break your addiction.

Perhaps you are fasting because there is something in your inner life that you need to conquer. Or maybe there is something in your world that you need to overcome. So you fast to get God's help to conquer yourself or get victory over your world. And what do you get when you have become a conqueror? You get rest. Rest is that quality of God that you appropriate when you spend time in fasting and seeking His heart. You put aside food and the pursuit of physical satisfaction to search for the presence of God. Those who have never properly fasted have probably never attained this level of peace.

God promises you rest. If you are a slave to an addiction, you can be suddenly set free. Not only will you see yourself as free, but you will feel it and know it internally. You will rest in your freedom. Do you need rest? Have you been a slave to addiction? Why don't you fast to find rest in the Lord.

To Take Away

Rest is a wonderful anticipation to those who are so tired they can hardly stand up. Every ache in their body cries out for rest. And when rest finally comes, it's such a relief that they usually drift into sleep. Unfortunately then, the experience of rest is gone because while sleeping they are not aware of anything.

The greatest thing about rest is its anticipation, not its realization. Isn't that true about a lot of things in life? God gives us the anticipation of rest to help us get through the drudgery of pain along the journey.

One day we will have perfect...soothing...snoozing... rest. I can hardly wait! But there's something greater than rest, it's God Himself. One day we'll have the passion of our hearts—perfect communion with God.

NOTES

Resting

Chapter 10

KNOWING

*But the people that do know their God shall be strong,
and do exploits* (Daniel 11:32b).

*This is what the Lord says: Let not the wise man boast
of his wisdom or the strong man boast of his strength
or the rich man boast of his riches, but let him who
boasts boast about this: that he understands and
knows Me* (Jeremiah 23-24a NIV).

I t is extremely important that your idea of God corre-
sponds to the true being of God. You can know about
Him conceptually in your head, but that is not enough.
You must also know Him relationally in your heart. Many
people learn a correct creed or statement about God, but
it is of little consequence to their daily life because they
live as though there is no God. What good is it to understand the real concept of God but bury it beneath theol-
ogy books and creedal statements?

How well do you know God? Most of us who have been converted can share our experience of what happened when we were saved. We rattle off our testimony and tell all about the things that happened to us. But during our profession, we fail to mention that we have come to know God personally and intimately.

The problem is that most of us want a formula to know Him. As if we put the right ingredients in the bowl, we can bake the perfect cake. Thus, we feel that if we apply the right formula, we automatically get to know God. Not so.

Searching to know God. Are you searching for God? Some search for Him in their head, and what they find is just a definition that describes God. Some search in their appetites and only find a God that is likened unto them. Others search for Him with their whole heart, and because their heart controls both their head and their hand, they are more likely than anyone else to find the actual true God. Why? You only find God when you search for Him with your whole heart.

And ye shall seek Me, and find Me, when ye shall search for Me with all your heart (Jeremiah 29:13).

Knowing other gods. Many people think they know the real God, but they have actually created an idol that has replaced God. An idol is nothing more than a man-made god carved from the fears of your fallen heart and has no likeness to the true God. No matter what god you make in place of the true God, no matter what your source for thinking about any god other than the true God, and no matter your motive, your false god always comes from your self-creation. We make our gods as much like ourselves as we can. Remember, God knows what we are doing for He said, "Thou thoughtest that I was altogether such an one as thyself..." (Ps. 50:21b). The gods of our darkened hearts are no gods at all.

Among all the commandments of God, the first is that we should have no other gods before Him, and there is nothing more hateful to God than idolatry. Why? You've made God something that He isn't. Idols are carved from an idolater's heart, and assumes that God is not the One who will judge us for rejecting Him. When we make gods after our own image and likeness, we are rejecting the God who made us after His image and likeness (see Gen. 1:26-27). And as we try to conform our god to our image, it is He who wants to conform us to His likeness. Oh, the monstrous evil of it all, when we assume God's place by trying to make Him like us; when at the same time, God is trying to make us like Him.

What did Paul say about idolaters? "...they glorified Him not as God, neither were thankful; but became vain in their imaginations, and their foolish heart was darkened" (Rom. 1:21). So where did we go wrong? It began in a blackened mind that had no light. So we fast to get more light...more understanding...more understanding of God. When you fast, you deny the ferocious appetite of your body to create a new appetite of your soul, an appetite to know God—to know Him correctly, to know Him personally, to know Him intimately. Lord, give me that appetite.

Why You Don't Know God
1. **Your mind is influenced by worldliness.**
2. **Your mind tends to doubt because of skepticism.**
3. **Your mind is confused because of humanism.**
4. **You believe God is not here.**
5. **You believe God does not care.**

Knowing God can solve your problems. Have you ever realized that knowing God will solve thousands of your everyday troubles and worries? When you find God, you have found the only One who can solve every one of your irritating problems.

When you look behind the source of every crushing weight, you will ultimately find that all trouble comes from sin. Traced all the way back to the Garden of Eden, sin has always destroyed our relationship with God, and it keeps us from knowing God, the only one who can help us get out of the mess we are in.

God can help you, but when you reject Him, He allows your problems to weigh you down and pulverize you. He patiently waits for you to come to Him, all the while knowing your pain is killing you. Why does a loving God do this? Anguish is often the only way to get your attention and turn your heart toward Him. In love He allows pain to motivate you to know Him, because it is then He can shower His love upon you. The crushing weight of all of life is nothing more than a solitary call to repentance; it is a mighty weight from God Himself. *God, help me see Your hand in my troubles.*

When you begin to know God, you begin to understand how to solve your problems and lift the weight from your shoulders. Of course, in this life we will never completely rid ourselves of difficulties, but we can find some relief in God Himself. Sometimes even then, the crushing burden of circumstances remains heavy on your shoulders; but when you know God, they are no longer heavy, even though they remain.

Knowing God can eliminate every cancer from your mind, and transform ashes into beauty. When you come to fully understand God—high and lifted up—nothing else matters in life. An elevated view of God changes your perspective, while an inaccurate view of God corrupts all your thoughts. *Lord, I want to know You.*

Knowing God intimately. When Daniel said, "But the people that do know their God shall be strong, and do exploits" (Dan. 11:32b, emphasis mine), he used the Hebrew word yadà, which means more than acquaintance or casual knowledge. Daniel is not telling us to know about God; He is describing intimate knowledge as you become one intimately with God. The term yadà is the same word used for sexual intimacy—"And Adam knew Eve his wife; and she conceived" (Gen. 4:1a, see also verse 25). I am not saying to know God is likened to having sex; I am saying it has the same results. When you know God intimately, it is similar to the results when a man knows his wife intimately,

"They shall be one flesh" (Gen. 2:24b). When you know God intimately, it is becoming one with Him. He knows you and you know Him. While you both have separate identities, you become one in spirit.

I have lived with my wife, Ruth, for 49 years as I write this chapter. I know her intimately; I know what she likes to eat when she goes to a restaurant, and I know what restaurants she prefers. I know things like how she talked with our children and how she both punished and rewarded them. As a matter of fact, I know my wife so well we can talk without using words. The other day I asked her, "Did you get the...?" Before I could finish my request she answered, "Yes, it's in the garage." I followed up with another question, "What about the...?" And before I could finish my second question she answered, "Yes, it's also in the garage." I was going to ask her about getting the lawn mower and the gas so I could cut the grass. She knew what I wanted to do, when I wanted to do it, and what I needed to get the job done. When you are so intimate that you are one, you will know what another asks even before the words are communicated.

Knowing God can be described in four pictures. Knowing God is like a son knowing his father; second, like a wife knowing her husband; third, like sheep knowing their shepherd; and finally, like followers knowing the king. Three relationships are portrayed by these pictures. First, to know is to look up to the other one with respect. Second, the person you know takes responsibility for your welfare. Finally, the person, like God, allows himself to be known.

How well do you know God? Do you merely know about God, or are you one intimately with God? *Lord, make me one with You.*

Knowing God builds strength. Let's go back to our original Bible verse at the beginning of this chapter. "But the people that do know their God shall be strong, and do exploits" (Dan. 11:32b). In the original language, *exploits* means to "work effectively." That means you will become successful or victorious in difficult situations. The Hebrew word for strong (hazak) means ability to endure the race or ability to resist temptations. When you know God, you can fend for yourself. When you know God, you can resist strange temptations in this crazy world.

Be careful that you're not seeking to know God just to be "toughed up." If you have any selfish or dishonest desire to know God, you have deceived yourself. "The man who thinks he knows something does not yet know as he ought to know" (1 Cor. 8:2 NIV).

To Take Away

We know God because He took the initiative to first know us. God told Jeremiah, "Before I formed you in the womb I knew you, before you were born I set you apart" (Jer. 1:5a NIV). God could tell Moses, "I am pleased with you and I know you by name" (Ex. 33:17b NIV).

We can know God by faith because He sent His Son to die for us. He took the initiative before we ever desired to know Him. *Thank You, Lord, for seeking me.*

To know God, You must come to Him through Jesus Christ who said, "I am the way and the truth and the life. No one comes to the Father except through Me" (Jn. 14:6 NIV).

Jesus knew us long before we came to know Him. He said, "I am the good shepherd; I know My sheep and My sheep know Me...I lay down My life for the sheep...My sheep listen to My voice; I know them...they shall never perish..." (Jn. 10:14-15,27-28 NIV). Because He first knew us, we can know Him. *Lord, I want to know You better.*

NOTES

Additional copies of this book and other
book titles from DESTINY IMAGE are
available at your local bookstore.

For a complete list of our titles,
visit us at www.destinyimage.com
Send a request for a catalog to:

Destiny Image® Publishers, Inc.
P.O. Box 310
Shippensburg, PA 17257-0310

*"Speaking to the Purposes of God for This
Generation and for the Generations to Come"*